LEWIS GRIZZARD

ON THE SOUTH

LEWIS GRIZZARD

O N   T H E   S O U T H

SOUTHERN

by the Grace of God

Edited by Gerrie Ferris

LONGSTREET PRESS, INC.
Atlanta, Georgia

Published by LONGSTREET PRESS, INC.,
a subsidiary of Cox Newspapers,
a division of Cox Enterprises, Inc.
2140 Newmarket Parkway
Suite 118
Marietta, Georgia 30067

Printed in the United States of America

1st printing, 1996

Library of Congress Catalog Number 95-82236

ISBN: 1-56352-279-9

Jacket design by Neil Hollingsworth
Book design by Jill Dible

LEWIS GRIZZARD

O N   T H E   S O U T H

BORN RIGHT

ALL OF US NATIVE SOUTHERNERS KNEW IT WAS COMING.
And now, it is here. The Sunday paper carried a large article
about Northern migration to the capital city of the
South.

In the metro Atlanta area, the article said, native Georgians still have the edge, but it's not an overpowering one
and the margin is dwindling. Said the article, "The migration patterns that brought Northeasterners to Atlanta's elite
northern suburbs also sent people from other regions to
spots around the metro area. These settling patterns . . .
have brought a new sense of place to dozens of Atlanta
neighborhoods, influencing everything from local politics
to the inventory at the corner grocery store."

The article also quoted a Yankee population expert,
William Frey of the University of Michigan, as saying, "The
nice Southern flavor of Atlanta may be diluted a bit with all
the Northerners moving in."

The nice Southern flavor of Atlanta may be diluted a
bit . . . .

I certainly understand why somebody from the land of

freeze and squeeze would want to seek asylum here. A friend, also a native Southerner, who shares my fear about losing our Southern flavor, put it this way: "Nobody is going into an Atlanta bar tonight celebrating because they've just been transferred to New Jersey."

So what should I expect as my beloved Southland becomes more populated with migrating honkers? (Honker: Northerner with a grating accent who always talks at the top of his or her voice.) Will Southerners start dropping the last part of everybody's first name like the honkers do? Will I forever be Lew? Will Mary become Mare? Will Nancy become Nance? Will Bubba become Bub?

Will the automobile horn drown out the lilt of "Georgia on My Mind"? Will they dig a tunnel through Stone Mountain so native New Yorkers can remember the dark, choking atmosphere of the Lincoln and the Holland Tunnels? Will Harold's barbecue, 45 years in the business, lose its clientele to delicatessens where you have to scream at the top of your voice to get somebody to take your order for pastrami on pumpernickel?

Will the downtown Atlanta statue of the Phoenix, symbolic of the city's rising from the ashes, be replaced by a statue of Sherman holding a can of lighter fluid? Will grits become extinct? Will corn bread give way to the bagel? Will everybody, including native Southerners, start calling Atlanta's pro football team the "Fall-cuns" like Yankee sportscasters, instead of the way it's supposed to be pronounced, "Fowl-cuns?"

Will "freeway" replace "expressway"? Will "soda" or "pop" replace "Co-coler"? Will Southern men start wearing black socks and sandals with Bermuda shorts? Will "Y'all come back" become "Git outta here"?

I was having lunch at an Atlanta golf club recently. A man sitting at another table heard me speaking and asked, "Where are you all from?" He was mocking me. He was mocking my Southern accent. He was sitting in Atlanta, Georgia, making fun of the way I speak.

He was from Toledo. He had been transferred to Atlanta. If I hadn't have been 46 years old, skinny, and a basic coward with a bad heart, I'd have punched him. I did, however, give him a severe verbal dressing down.

I was in my doctor's office in Atlanta. One of the women who works there, a transplanted Northerner, asked how I pronounced the world "siren." I said I pronounced it "si-reen." I was half kidding, but that is the way I heard the word pronounced when I was a child.

The woman laughed and said, "You Southerners really crack me up. You have a language all your own."

Yeah, we do. If you don't like it, go back home and stick your head in a snow bank. We really don't care how you said it or how you did it back in Buffalo.

I read a piece on the op-ed page of the *Constitution* written by somebody who in the jargon of my past "ain't from around here." He wrote white Southerners are always looking back and that we should look forward. He said that about me. He was reacting to a bumper sticker that shows the old Confederate soldier saying, "FERGIT HELL!"

I don't go around sulking about the fact that the South lost the Civil War. But I am aware that once upon a long time ago, a group of Americans saw fit to rebel against what they thought was an overbearing federal government. There is no record anywhere that indicates anybody in my family living in 1861 owned slaves. As a matter of fact, I come from a long line of sharecroppers, horse thieves, and used car dealers. But a few of them fought anyway — not to keep their slaves, because they didn't have any. I guess they simply thought it was the right thing to do at the time.

Whatever their reasons, there was a citizenry that once saw fit to fight and die and I come from all that, and I look at those people as brave and gallant, and a frightful force until their hearts and their lands were burnt away.

I will never turn my back on that heritage. I am proud to be a Southerner. If I've said it once, I've said it a thousand times: I'm an American by birth, but I'm Southern by the grace of God.

PUT SOME SOUTH IN YO' MOUTH

Look Away, Look Away, and Watch What You Say

As soon as Bill Clinton was elected president, along with his running mate Al Gore, I knew "y'all" would be thrust upon the public like white on grits.

Clinton, of course, is from Arkansas and Gore is from Tennessee. I don't count either man as having all the characteristics of a true Southerner, since both passed up their state universities for Georgetown and the Ivy League.

But both obviously understand "y'all" and use it often. "Y'all" is, to be sure, a Southern thing that most people living outside the South don't understand.

I have long been involved in y'allism. I find it a charming word that is pure Southern, but because it is so often misunderstood, I thought it would be wise to discuss "y'all" at some length.

The biggest mistake people from outside the South make in the y'all area is they don't think we say "y'all" at all. They think we say "you all."

A Southerner visiting the North surely will be mocked the first time he or she opens his or her mouth and out comes a Southern accent.

Northerners will giggle and ask, "So where are you all from?" I answer by saying, "I all is from Atlanta."

For some unknown reason, Northerners think Southerners use "you all" in the singular sense. How many movies have I seen where a Northerner is trying to do a Southern accent, failing miserably, saying you all, while addressing one other person?

Southerners rarely use "you all" in any situation but they never, never, ever, ever, use it when addressing just one person. If you were in my home and I offered you a cup of coffee I would say, "Would you like a cup of coffee?" If you and your brother-in-law and your cousin were in my home, then I'd say, "Would y'all like a cup of coffee?"

"Y'all" is, of course, a contraction of "you all," and most Southerners use it in all verbal situations involving more than one other person.

And another thing: Northerners also tend to think Southerners say the following when bidding a farewell to a visitor: "You all come back now, you heah?" Maybe the Clampetts said that, but very few real Southerners do.

We might say, "Y'all come back to see us when you can," or, "If y'all can't come, call."

But this "you heah" business is the concoction of some Yankee scriptwriter trying to be cute.

I rarely get into a punching mode, but I was in New York doing a tape version of a book I had written and the producer had hired an actor to speak some of the lines.

"Can you do a Southern accent?" I asked the actor.

"Would you all like to hear me?" he answered.

"I've already heard enough," I said. Then I turned to the producer and said, "This man isn't going to be on my book tape because I will not have the Yankee version of Southern accent in or on anything that bears my name."

The actor became enraged and said he could, too, do a Southern accent, and I replied, "If you can do a Southern accent, pigs can fly."

We got into each other's face, but before we came to blows, the producer fired the man and ordered him out of the studio and the script was altered so I would be the only one speaking on the tape.

I take the Southern accent and the preservation of its purity quite seriously. And if any of y'all don't like it, just keep it to yourself, you heah?

Crossing the Mason-Diction Line

IT WAS THE 1991 POULAN WEEDEATER INDEPENDENCE Bowl between the Universities of Georgia and Arkansas, the Dawgs and the Hawgs respectively.

One would think television people wouldn't have a problem repeating the above paragraph correctly, but that hasn't been the case, and so once again I must assume my role as Slim Pickens, Professor of Speaking Correctly.

Let us begin with Poulan. A local announcer pronounced it POH-land, as in the Eastern European country. (Not as in the recession-ridden United States.) It's POO-lahn, I think. What the announcer should have done anyway is not try to say Poulan at all, but simply call it the Weedeater Bowl.

I like a football game named after such an aggressive piece of equipment as the weedeater. A coach could say, "Boys, they're grass and we're a bunch of souped-up Weedeaters."

Coaches say things like that, as well as things like, "Remember, boys, they put their pants on one leg at a time, just like we do."

Whenever a coach said something like that to me, I always thought, "Well, I guess so. Who the hell could jump into a pair of pants two legs at a time?" I'm certain it's POO-lahn, and if it's not, it should be. The professor has the last word.

Now, to Dawgs and Hawgs.

A dawg is a Southern man's best friend, as in, "That dawg'll hunt."

A hawg is Southern for, "You can lead a hawg to water, but all he'll try to do is waller in it."

But I was watching a network telecast of the Atlanta–New Orleans NFL playoff game recently and one of the announcers was hyping the telecast of the Independence Bowl. It came out: "It's the Dugs and the Hugs in the Independence Bowl."

It was quite obvious the announcer wasn't, as they used to say back home, "from 'round heah," which basically meant he was a Northerner.

Read my lips: "Dawwwwwgs." Put your tongue to the roof of your mouth. Then bring it down forcibly and spit out "Dawwwwwgs" by forming the mouth into a circle. If it comes out a little nasal, more the better.

For "Hawwwwwgs," it comes from deep in the throat as in "Haw!" Pretend you're spitting out a bad oyster.

Some announcers also say the Atlanta "FALL-cuns." It's "FOWL-cans." And they say "aw-BURN" when they should pronounce it "AW-bun."

Television, I believe, is responsible for the slow disappearance of all sorts of accents in this country. I'm afraid one day everybody will sound alike, and that would be a shame.

Professor Grizzard would be out of work, and who

would care about an athletic event between the Dugs and the Hugs? Sounds more like an encounter group than a bunch of fired-up weedeaters trying to take each other's heads off, which builds character both on and off the field.

The Dawgs and the Hawgs. It's a Southern thing. The rest of y'all just wouldn't understand.

I Wish I Was . . .
Politically Correct in Dixie

I CERTAINLY AGREE WITH ALL THOSE WHO HAVE PROTESTED the playing of "Dixie" at Southern football games.

Although slavery isn't mentioned in the song, it still makes people think of the Old South, where every white person owned African-American slaves.

"Dixie" is definitely a politically incorrect piece of music. Even the word is offensive to some, and I apologize to those who are offended by my use of it.

But I'm proud to say my alma mater, the University of Georgia, years ago rid itself of any connection with the song or the word you-know-what (see, I didn't use the word that time, as I despise offending people).

The Georgia band used to play the song at football games. But not anymore. The only place they still play the song is at the University of Mississippi. They also wave Confederate flags and they allow prayer before a football game.

I'm not certain how long it will be before members of the Speech Police move in and shut down such reprehensible behavior, but it could be any day now.

Georgia not only stopped playing the song, it even changed the name of the band, formerly known as the Dixie Redcoat Band. It became simply the Redcoat Band.

That prompted my stepbrother, Ludlow Porch, the

famous radio talk show personality, to fire off a letter to the editor suggesting the following: "I applaud the dropping of 'Dixie' from the name of the University of Georgia band, but let us not stop there.

"How can we allow the word 'red,' which stands for communism? And the word 'redcoat' itself is an affront to the memory of all those Americans who fought against the redcoats of England in the Revolutionary War.

"And 'band.' Poncho Villa had a 'band' of desperadoes and we had to send brave young soldiers into Mexico after him. So 'band' should go, too, and that just leaves 'The,' which is a dumb name for a large number of musicians, so I guess they're just out of a name altogether."

I believe if we really try we can wipe away all symbols of the Old South forever. There's a company in Savannah that makes Dixie Crystal Sugar. Sorry, it's just Crystal Sugar from now on, and don't give me any grief about it.

And there's even a Dixie Highway in the South. It should be referred to from now on only as Highway. As in, "Well, you take Highway, then go down three blocks and. . . ." There are even some people named Dixie, believe it or not. They will have to get new first names, or go by their middle names. And if anybody named Dixie lives on Dixie Highway, the Speech Police will likely demand they be shot.

And if the song and word "Dixie" are symbolic of the Old South, I guess we ought to stop using "Old South" as well. Instead of saying "Old South" perhaps we can refer to it as "Back Then," and we can roll our eyes when we use it so everybody will know we aren't talking about when dinosaurs roamed the Earth, but when slaveholders used to go around singing songs like "Dixie" and "Eating Goober Peas."

But wait. "Eating Goober Peas" is a song from Back Then, too, so don't anybody dare play that at a football game.

Rap songs about killing innocent people, incidentally, are just fine.

No Offense,
but I Am Taking Offense

I'M OFFENDED.

I never thought I would say that because I'm an easy-going type of guy who figures it's a lot less stressful not to let anybody get to me.

But these are the '90s, and getting offended is "in," like drinking bottled water, refusing to eat red meat, and cursing smokers.

Hardly a day passes that somebody doesn't make the news by getting offended.

Sister Souljah, the rap person, rapped about killing white people, and then she became offended because Bill Clinton said she was a racist for doing such a thing.

Jesse Jackson, who was born offended, also got offended by Mr. Clinton's remarks, so it was a 2-on-1 fastbreak, two offendees on one offender. Hardly sounds fair, but that's baseball these days.

And that brings up Native Americans becoming offended by Atlanta Braves fans' tomahawk chop and criminals becoming offended by the name Texas Rangers, since Texas Rangers are law enforcement people who nab a lot of criminals and send them to jail.

So why should I be left off the bandwagon of offendees? It's a free country, isn't it? Here's why I'm offended.

There was an article on the front page of the Atlanta

newspaper the other day concerning suburban Clayton
County promoting itself as a nice place to live in order to
persuade more Atlanta area people to move there.

The second paragraph began: "Feeling that the county
has been treated for years as metro Atlanta's redneck
stepchild. . . ."

That offended me.

In the first place, I know the origin of the term "redneck," and several members of my family fell into that cat-
egory.

"Redneck" got its start when ruralites came to town on
Saturdays to buy feed, seed and maybe a new pair of bro-
gans.

These people made their living working in the fields
under the hot sun growing food, a very worthwhile endeav-
or, and their necks often became sunburned.

Townfolk, who tend to be snooty, thought these people
ignorant, uncouth and undesirable because they tended to
drive pickup trucks, to listen to the Grand Ol' Opry on the
radio on Friday nights, and to be humble.

They were easy to pick on, in other words. My grandfather was one of those people. He made his living from
behind a mule, and his neck got red. He also liked Ernest
Tubb, and I never heard him make a loud, bodacious statement of any kind.

He also was the most gentle, caring person I've ever
known, and I'm glad he didn't live long enough to see the

term applied to him become such a derisive label.

In the second place let us discuss the term "stepchild."

In the context it was used — redneck stepchild — it seemed to indicate someone of that description was a most undesirable individual.

I spring from those who worked the soil and became red of neck, and I had a stepfather, so I was a stepchild, and that makes me twice offended.

Now, if you'll excuse me, I'm going to ride around in my red Blazer — a sort of pickup truck — and pout.

"Bubba Bashers" Use Stereotype That Doesn't Fit

FOR YEARS, I HAVE ATTEMPTED TO ENLIGHTEN THOSE INDI-viduals who hold biased and ill-based opinions about the name "Bubba."

Most think men named Bubba are nothing more than ignorant swine who wear caps with the names of heavy equipment dealers on the front, shoot anything that moves, listen to music about doing bodily harm to hippies and put beer on their grits.

There may be Bubbas who fit the above description, but there are plenty who don't.

I once wrote of a man college-educated, with no tobac-co juice stains on his teeth, whose family had always referred to him as Bubba.

"I got that name," he explained, "because my baby sister couldn't say brother. She called me Bubba."

The man's problem was that he had taken a job with some sort of high-tech corporation, and his boss insisted he drop the name "Bubba" because he thought clients would-n't respect a man with such a name. Our Bubba refused to use any other name, however, and became quite successful with his new company and wound up with his former boss's job. The former boss now refers to his old employee as "Mr. Bubba."

Anyway, I happened to pick up a back issue of *Southern*

magazine recently, and on the very front cover were the following words: "Bubba! You don't have to be dumb, mean, fat, slow, white or male to be one!"

I turned to page 37 and began to read: "Of all the Southern stereotypes," the story began, "the one that answers to 'Bubba' is probably the least flattering."

The article went on to do portraits of eight Bubbas. Do any of the following fit the typical "Bubba stereotype"?

Keith "Bubba" Taniguche: lawyer, Austin, Texas. Full-blooded Japanese. Into Zen.

John "Bubba" Trotman: state director of the U.S. Agriculture Department's Agricultural Stabilization and Conservation Service, Montgomery, Alabama. On people moving into Alabama: "At first, they say, 'Alabama, that's Tobacco Road.' Then you can't blow them out of Alabama with a cannon."

Efula "Bubba" Johnson: narcotics officer, Savannah, Georgia. Johnson is a large man, and he carries a large gun.

Walter "Bubba" Smith: minister, Ashdown, Arkansas. Claims no relation to Bubba Smith of football and beer commercial fame.

James "Bubba" Armstrong: surgeon, Montgomery, Alabama. Careful poking fun at anybody who knows his way around a scalpel.

Paula "Bubba" Meiner: owns a barbecue joint in Winter Park, Florida. Nice lady.

Bernard "Bubba" Meng: state administrator for U.S.

Senator Ernest Hollings. Columbia, South Carolina. He's "Little Bubba." Dad was "Big, etc."

Kyle "Bubba" Patrick: elementary school student, Auburntown, Tennessee. He wants to be a basketball player when he grows up.

One more thing: The University of Georgia veterinary school produced the state's first test-tube calf, a Holstein bull, weighing 100 pounds.

They named him Bubba. What else?

U.S. of the South Still a Good Idea?

AN ATLANTA *JOURNAL-CONSTITUTION* SURVEY HAS UNCOV-
ered the rather astounding fact that one in five lifelong
Southerners still thinks the South should be its own
nation.

This is even more astounding: The poll also indicated 27
percent of black Southerners "lean toward Southern independence."

That's a lot of people. That's a lot more "Fergit, hell!"
bumper stickers than I would have thought.

"You would think the idea would have died by now but
it hasn't," the papers quoted Emory Thomas, a Civil War
historian at the University of Georgia.

I'll say. It's been 130 years since the Civil War. It's been
60 years since *Gone With the Wind* debuted in Atlanta.

What could all this mean? As far as the 27 percent of
black Southerners who favor independence, the Rev. Joseph
Lowery of the Southern Christian Leadership Conference
said he didn't think blacks understood the question.

"I can't see anybody seeing an advantage to the United
States of the Confederacy," he went on.

But maybe they can.

I don't think you would find many white Southerners
and certainly no black Southerners who would want to
return to a slave state, but perhaps this has to do with something else.

Many of us Southerners might think we could simply do
a lot better on our own if we didn't have Washington and

New York and that Eastern corridor of arrogance and eggheadedness with which to deal.

The rest of the North I don't really worry about. We probably even would let Minnesota into the new confederacy if it weren't so cold.

But what has Washington ever done for us in the South besides take our money, close our military bases, use us for a dump and foul up our schools? If we were the United States of the South, we wouldn't have to deal with Bill and Hillary anymore, either, and I still don't consider them Southern even if they are from Arkansas.

They both went to Yale and couldn't identify a razorback hog if it walked into the White House.

And New York? Why do we need to be in the same country with New York?

They think we're still one big pellagra belt and we're not even sure New York could still qualify as an American city. Try to find a cabdriver who speaks English or a dope dealer who can tell you the name of one co-signer of the Declaration of Independence in New York. The more I think of this concept, the more I like it.

There would be immediate problems, of course. What to do about South Florida would be one. It's about as Southern as wearing black socks with Bermuda shorts and sandals. And could the Yankees already living there pass citizenship tests? Would they stop wearing black socks with Bermuda shorts and sandals? But at least we could tighten the immigration laws and keep a lot more out. Yankees aren't bad people, but you have to spend a lot of time dressing them correctly and explaining we never use "you all" in the singular.

This has some exciting possibilities, like putting the new capitol in Little Rock just for spite.

Chicago-Like Weather Chills Urge to Gloat

WAIT A MINUTE. IF I HAD WANTED TO CONTINUE TO LIVE like Nanook of the North, I'd never have packed my sled and moved back South from Chicago years ago.

I spent three winters in Gulag Chicago. One year, Lake Michigan froze solid. Another year, it snowed in May. The third year, the heat went off, and my apartment froze. My entire apartment. My clothes froze. My furniture froze. I froze.

I had to move downstairs with my landlord. His heat went off, too, but he had a wood-burning stove. We huddled around the stove for a week.

Finally, he said, "This is ridiculous. I'm moving to Orlando."

"You're right," I said. "I'm moving back to Atlanta."

So I did. Back to the sunny South. One of the best parts about getting out of Chicago was I knew I would never have to wear a pair of galoshes again.

You have to wear galoshes over your regular shoes during Chicago winters. If you don't, your shoes will fill up with snow and your toes will freeze and fall off.

Just fall right off. Imagine life without toes. There would be precious little left to wiggle.

The problem with galoshes is they look dumb. Seriously dumb.

The only Southerners who wear galoshes are nerds whose mothers came from up North somewhere.

These mothers give their children names such as Manny, and Vito, and Melvin and say, "Melvin, don't forget to wear your galoshes," when their children leave for school.

It doesn't matter if the sun is shining and it's 70° outside, a nerd whose mother is from up North and still hasn't got over it will insist he wear his galoshes, and the other students will throw rocks at him and hoot him off the playground.

Another great part about moving back South is, although we do have a winter, it doesn't last nearly as long and isn't nearly as severe as in Chicago.

I've played tennis outdoors while wearing shorts on Christmas Day in Atlanta.

Atlanta usually has an ice storm or two in January, but by the middle of February you often can go outside and catch a few rays.

But what's with this year? I looked in the paper the other day, and it was just as cold in Atlanta as it was in Chicago. That just isn't right.

I also noticed it was snowing in Florida. That just isn't right, either. It's not supposed to snow in Florida. Isn't that in the Bible someplace? I don't know what meteorological aberration has caused the South to have to suffer through these Chicago-like temperatures lately, but I would just as soon it stop.

For one thing, I'm missing my annual gloating period. During winter, I look at a color weather map in the newspaper. I notice it's white in Chicago, which means your toes could fall off if you don't wear galoshes. Then, I notice the South is a pleasant warm orange. I still have friends in

Chicago. I call them and gloat.

"So," I usually begin, "got enough whale blubber in to last the winter?" That, or, "Getting out of the igloo much?" I usually close by saying, "Hey, it's been real, but I'm late for my neighbor's pool party."

But how can I gloat when I think I saw a penguin waddling down Peachtree Street the other day? Not only am I missing my gloating period, but I'm also afraid if it doesn't warm up soon, I may have to search through the bowels of my closet to see if I still have my galoshes, a fate worse than death. I honestly never thought I'd have to wear a pair of galoshes again. But I also never thought the normally mild early winter of the South would be gone with the arctic wind.

Y'all, Let's Teach Yankees a Lesson

SOUTHERN READERS RECENTLY HAVE FLOODED ME WITH copies of articles written in Northern newspapers concerning Atlanta and the Olympics, the Braves in the World Series, the tomahawk chop and the fact that Ted Turner and wife, Jane Fonda, dozed off during one of the Braves' playoff games against the Pirates.

Much of it is the same old tripe, with the worn references to Bubba, the Southern accent, General Sherman and Petticoat Junction.

There even was a reference to me, saying I was a cross between Buck Owens and David Letterman. It could have been worse. They could have called me a cross between Boxcar Willie and Pat Sajak.

I continue to protest such stereotypical references to the land I love, and it's interesting that a Northern transplant to the South, in a letter to the editor, compared me to David Duke as a spreader of geographical hatred.

So what does that make Twin Cities columnist Nick Coleman, who wrote, "Somebody has made off with these people's [Atlantans'] brains"? Sadly, the Chicago *Tribune's* Mike Royko fell victim to all this, as well.

The reason I use the word "sadly" is because Mike Royko is my idol.

I consider him to be the best newspaper columnist in America.

I've never met Mike Royko, but I did have the pleasure of reading him the three years I lived in Chicago, and I still search for his syndicated column when I travel.

Royko is hilarious. He is inventive. He can take out your appendix with a broken Budweiser bottle.

He took offense to the instance of Ted and Jane going to sleep in Ted's private box at Atlanta–Fulton County Stadium.

"True baseball fans stay awake, even the drunks," he wrote. "So these two snoozers don't deserve a world champion team."

He wasn't through.

"Nor do the fans in Atlanta with their Indian tomahawk chop and the terrible noise they make, like a giant herd of pregnant moo-cows."

I could have lived with most of that, especially the part about Ted and Jane going to sleep during a playoff game. What I have against Ted Turner is he married Hanoi Jane, and what I have against her isn't going to get in this column.

But then Royko takes off on the Southern accent with a trite explanation of how we say "snowin" instead of "snoring" and "mowf" instead of "mouth."

He also makes fun of the way the Puerto Ricans pronounce "Blue Jay" and one wonders where all the politically correct editors in Chicago have gone.

Mike Royko is better than all that. He must have tarried too long at Billy Goat's Tavern.

I also received a clip from *USA Today*. Somebody named Taylor Buckley was perplexed about golf being considered for the 1996 Atlanta Summer Olympics as a "signature" event.

Writes he, "Why not 'signature' in these games with a

genuine Bubba sport? Like a monster-truck tug of war, complete with Confederate flags, gun racks and trucks named 'Dixie Dawg Kicker' and 'Roadkill Rebel?'" Those readers who took offense to all this asked me to write a rebuttal.

I've got a better idea: Let's win the World Series again, put on a marvelous 1996 Summer Olympics and if you're traveling through the North and see a state flag, turn it upside down.

Call Me Violent? I'll Buy a Knife!

HERE AT THE SOUTHERN ANTI-DEFAMATION LEAGUE, WE
have received yet another example of what I believe to be a
continuing, unwarranted attack upon Southerners and
their lifestyles from other parts of the country.

An alert reader sent along an article out of *Psychology
Today* concerning a study by a University of Michigan
researcher who has concluded Southerners are more violent
than Northerners.

Richard E. Nisbett, Ph.D., says Southerners are more
likely than Northerners to resort to violence when insulted.
He says that makes the South "a hotbed of homicide."

And why are we so touchy? "All the violence stems not
from some intrapsychic source, but a cultural code of honor
borne of a pig-herding past," concludes Mr. PhDuckBrain.
He continues, "It's the legacy of Scotch-Irish settlers who
brought with them the tough defensive stance herders the
world over assume to protect their livelihood from rustlers."

Well, I guess so. Somebody steals your pig, what are you
supposed to do? Look him up and ask him to dance? And
if indeed Southerners are a little quick-tempered about an
insult, it's because we've been insulted by the rest of the
country long enough.

I'm tired of being referred to as a "bubba," a "redneck"
and worse.

Damn straight. Some Northern greaseball (if you can call
me a redneck, I can call you a greaseball) gets on my case,
then, in the immortal words of my boyhood friend and

idol, Weyman C. Wannamaker, he'll have to settle the matter with "me and King Hardware."

King Hardware was the concern back home where one might purchase a knife.

You want to talk about Michigan, home of Mr. PhDonkey. OK. I recently received another letter from William L. Nix, an attorney in West Point, Georgia. He told of a trip he and his wife and two sons took to the Upper Peninsula of Michigan. The family stopped for dinner at a Red Lobster at Jackson, Michigan.

The waitress asked the two boys if they would like to see a children's menu. Both boys answered, "Yes, ma'am."

"Like all self-respecting Southerners," wrote attorney Nix, "we have taught our children to say 'please,' 'thank you,' 'yes, ma'am and 'no, ma'am.' After our meal, our waitress said, 'You folks are from the South, aren't you?' I proudly replied that we were and inquired if it was our accents that she noticed.

"She said, 'No, it's just that your kids have manners. The kids up here are brats.'" William Nix ended with, "I relate this story not because my kids have exemplary manners. They don't. But it points out the fundamental difference between our way of life and theirs. Gentility and common courtesy still mean something to us. Let's hope it remains that way."

The reader who sent in the *Psychology Today* article asked me, "Are you going to take this lying down?" Getting out of my usually genteel mode, for a moment, I must say, not a chance. And I hope to kiss a pig if I ever do.

I'm disgusted at Southern smearing. I think Mr.

PhDumb's research is a farce and as Weyman also used to say, "As long as King Hardware stays open, I ain't budging an inch."

Frankly, My Dear, I Don't Understand

LET ME SEE IF I HAVE ALL THIS STRAIGHT: THREE METRO Atlanta counties — Clayton, Douglas and Henry — are all bidding for a $30 million *Gone With the Wind* theme park.

At the same time, an Atlanta foundation is conducting a fund-raising campaign to restore a building where Margaret Mitchell, who wrote *GWTW*, once lived.

Margaret Mitchell House Inc. needs $1 million to $3 million to restore what Ms. Mitchell called "The Dump" on Crescent Avenue and Peachtree Street.

Supporters of the renovation are even planning to try to raise money in Japan. "They adore *GWTW* in Japan," said a spokesperson for the Margaret Mitchell House.

OK. All that's fine. Nobody's complaining. *Gone With the Wind* is important to Atlanta's heritage and Margaret Mitchell is our most beloved literary figure.

Gone With the Wind, of course, is about plantation life in the Old South.

There were all those magnificent balls. And the happy slaves were singing in the cotton fields.

Then the Yankees came, burning and plundering. Miss Scarlet even had to shoot one of them and a way of life was gone forever. But certainly not its memory. *Gone With the Wind* has assured that, and we never want to forget.

Thus the efforts for the theme park and Margaret Mitchell's former place of residence.

But what's this? The Georgia state flag reminds us of the

Old South, too. It is modeled after the old Confederate battle banner.

But the flag, it seems, is politically incorrect. How some lash out against it. Said a recent letter to the editor: "How can anyone honor a flag, conceived in such hatred, or respect a banner designed to symbolize segregation? Where is the sensitivity toward the feelings for Georgians of African descent?"

So how do Georgians of African descent feel about a theme park that would remind them of a time when their forebears were enslaved? How many African-American families would visit such a place? How many African Americans will be willing to donate a few bucks to make certain Margaret Mitchell's residence is spared? Symbols of the past.

How can we rage against one and not include the others? Isn't the Cyclorama in Grant Park a symbol, too? What about the carving of Robert E. Lee and other Confederate generals on the side of Stone Mountain? Shouldn't we raze the Cyclorama and remove the Stone Mountain carving or at least cover it until the Olympics are over? There is so much concern the Olympics are going to come to Atlanta in 1996 and there will still be references to our rebel days and ways.

There's Tara Boulevard named for the plantation in *Gone With the Wind,* for God's sake. Change that to Malcolm X Boulevard, if we want to name a thoroughfare for him as has been suggested.

There are a lot of Confederate dead buried in Atlanta cemeteries. What do we do about them? Dig them up and move them to the Okeefenokee swamp? Just think what might happen in a *GWTW* theme park. Somebody might try to play Dixie. Somebody might suggest park personnel wear Confederate gray. Could you pay for your admission in Confederate money? Certainly African Americans would be hired to work in a theme park. How would they feel surrounded by vestiges of the Old South?

Somebody set me right here. How can there be so much objection to the state flag and not one fiddle-dee-dee about a $30 million theme park or a restored home — both of which would assure old times are not forgotten? I'm not condoning and I'm not condemning. I've simply got an inquiring mind that wants to know.

HONKERS, SANDALS WITH SOCKS, AND OTHER ABNORMALITIES

Delta's Ready When You Are

LITHUANIA HAS VOTED FOR INDEPENDENCE FROM THE Soviet Union. Other Soviet provinces want the same thing. The sweet wind of freedom is blowing.

OK, then. What about the South seceding again? I realize it didn't work the first time we tried it, but the North wouldn't fight fairly. As it is told, that great Georgian and Confederate, Robert Toombs, was trying to recruit men to fight for the South at the outbreak of the Civil War.

"Why, we can beat the Yankees with cornstalks," he told an audience. After the war, Toombs was running for governor. During a campaign speech a voice cried out from the audience, "We listened to you when you said we could beat the Yankees with cornstalks. That was a lie, so why should we believe you now?"

Toombs replied, "We could have beaten the Yankees with cornstalks, but the SOBs wouldn't fight that way."

I don't think there would be any hostilities if the South should decide to secede again.

If we did it in the winter, how could anybody who lives where it's always blue on the weather map blame us? And any of the millions of Northerners who had the good sense to move South before the secession could gain their citizenship in the All-New-and-Improved South quite easily.

All they would have to do is agree to go to speech school and learn how to lose their Northern accents.

Think of what it would be like if the South broke away from the Union again.

No more heavy taxes to bail out decaying Northern cities. No more stupid federal regulators.

There would be a few things we'd have to agree to do in the spirit of becoming good neighbors with the North.

We would agree to be equal partners in the Persian Gulf — which is more than can be said about any other ally.

We would also agree to come to the North's rescue in case it needed help for something like moving Philadelphia to somewhere in southern Illinois to make room for a parking lot when all the parking spaces in New York were taken.

I'd make Atlanta the capital of the South this time. Richmond's too close to Washington.

I would want minorities to have a chance in all leadership roles.

The Atlanta Braves and Falcons wouldn't have to play the New York Mets or Giants anymore. The Falcons could play Tampa Bay every week and actually have a chance for a break-even season.

A man can dream, can't he?

Kooks of the Klan Fascinate Yankees

BIG-TIME MEDIA SEEMS OBSESSED BY THE KU KLUX KLAN. Give them anything that has a sheet or a pointed hat involved in it, and it's time to pull out all the stops.

David Duke wasn't about to be elected in Louisiana, but he was a former Klansman, so he wound up on front pages across the country.

And David Duke was a Southerner, as well. A white Southern male with a Ku Klux Klan background can get more press than Mario Cuomo flipping a coin to see if he's going to run for president and then putting off the decision again to go for two out of three.

The Northern media are especially fond of the Klan as the basis for a news story. It's their geographical ignorance showing. What many Northerners know of the South they learned watching *The Beverly Hillbillies* or *Mississippi Burning.*

I was on the phone with a New Yorker, and he asked me, "What time is it in Atlanta?"

"What time is it in New York?" I asked him back.

"4:30," he said.

"You're not going to believe this," I said, "but Atlanta is in the same time zone as New York. It's 4:30 here, too."

Where did he think Georgia was? Next to Texas? One of those talk-show hostesses came to Atlanta. Apparently she couldn't find any Southern left-handed lesbian cross-dressers who were being denied their right to marry goats, so she rounded up a few Klansmen, or people who said they were in the Klan in order to get on television.

Several years ago, Larry King came to Atlanta to do his show and I was asked to appear on the second half. The first half, Larry King interviewed some kook from the Klan.

"How can you do this to me, Larry?" I joked with him. "Everybody watching this show sees me following a nut in a robe and a pointed hat and they figure my outfit's in the cleaners or something."

The Klan hasn't had any influence in the South in decades. What few members remain are too stupid, for one thing. What wears robes and pointed hats and has three teeth? Fifty-eight members of the KKK — which is about how many you could turn up given a year, a gasoline credit card and a road map of the South.

During the horror of Atlanta's murdered and missing children experience in the early 1980s, the rest of the world wanted the Klan involved. A Northern reporter walked in my office one day and asked if I knew how to get in touch with Atlanta's grand wizard. "I'm certain the Klan is involved in this," he said.

"Call 1-800-GET-REAL," I told him.

But what a story it would have made had the Klan been involved. The Ku Klux Klan killing black children in Atlanta, which is in Georgia, which is in the South. Think of the books. Think of the movie starring Northern actors and actresses trying to fake Southern accents.

Forget the Klan. Want something to worry about? OK, how about black men murdering other black men day after day? Getting laid off from your job? The Soviet nuclear arsenal winding up in the wrong hands? Or, the fact that the booger you wound up with under the sheets last night has AIDS.

Even Klansmen probably have enough sense to use Kondoms.

New York, New Yuck for This Southerner

IN A RECENT COLUMN I WROTE THAT I HAD REFUSED AN invitation to spend a weekend in New York with friends. I didn't go. I explained I wasn't afraid of the terrorists. I just didn't want to be around that many New Yorkers for that long.

In case you didn't know, if I get around a lot of New Yorkers I suffer from a number of reactions.

First, my ears hurt because New Yorkers are loud. They grow up having to scream in order to be heard over other New Yorkers.

This all stems from the fact New Yorkers are the most opinionated people on earth and can never learn to listen.

Secondly, I become extremely nervous and frustrated around New Yorkers. That is because they all talk so loudly and they all talk at once with New York accents, so I can't make out anything they are saying.

Let's say I'm in New York riding the subway. I'm always afraid New Yorkers around me are saying something important like, "I think the train is on fire," and I can't understand them.

Also, under certain circumstances, I become embarrassed around New Yorkers because of what they are wearing.

I was at a golf resort in Tampa recently. All over the course were guys wearing long black socks with their golfing shorts. They had to be New Yorkers. Only New Yorkers would wear long black socks with a pair of golfing shorts. People from other parts of the country, especially the South, know you never wear black socks with any kind of shorts.

I tried to tell a New Yorker that once, but he couldn't hear me because he was screaming his opinion on various Third World issues at the time.

The column elicited some reaction. A perfect example came from an Atlanta woman who said she grew up on Long Island.

"Probably," she began, "you're afraid of New Yorkers because they have a breadth of knowledge that you obviously can't touch. I'm sorry you are so afraid of us."

The lady was correct concerning the fact I am afraid of New Yorkers. But it is not because of their breadth of knowledge.

I'm afraid I'll go deaf if I spend too much time around New Yorkers. I'm afraid I'll start screaming my opinion. I'm afraid I'll show up at the golf course wearing black socks with my golfing shorts and my friends will point at me and laugh at me and ask, "Where's your sandals?" That's something else New Yorkers do. When they are wearing shorts and black socks somewhere besides the golf course, like at the beach, they wear sandals, another fashion miscue.

To New Yorkers who will be further offended by this column, I have just one thing to say: So sue me.

Let's Run These Ideas up the State's Flag Pole

I'VE BEEN TRYING TO FIGURE OUT A COMPROMISE ON THE controversy regarding Georgia's state flag.

The controversy is that one side says that because the flag features part of the old Confederate flag, it symbolizes racial oppression and hatred and it will be an embarrassment to the state and the city if it isn't changed before the 1996 Olympic Games in Atlanta.

The other side says all the Confederate flag is doing on the state flag is offering a symbol of the state's heritage. I can understand that. My great-great-grandfather, General Beauregard Grizzard, was in charge of keeping the Yankees out of Miami Beach during the Civil War.

And the two sides continue to go round and round. Somebody thought maybe the governor could figure this out.

But when asked his thoughts, Governor Zell Miller said he had a lot of other things more important than the state flag to handle.

I've used that sidestep myself when one of my ex-wives asked me where I'd been until 3:30 the previous morning. I said, "Don't bother me with little stuff like that. I'm try-ing to figure out who to pull for in the Iran-Iraq war."

But I've always been big on compromise. If I can't scream louder or argue the other side down, and if hitting them over the head with a baseball bat is out of the question because they're bigger than me, I go for compromise every time.

So let's see what we've got here: We've got a state flag that is causing divisiveness. What do we do? The most logical thing to me would be simply not to have a state flag. What does a state need a flag for? If Georgia ever decided to invade South Carolina and try to get Hilton Head back from all the Yankees who have moved there, we might need a state flag under which to march.

But I think it's too late to save Hilton Head. I was there recently and ordered grits for my breakfast. The waitress said, "Where do you think you are buddy, down South? With eggs you get potatoes."

But why else would we need a state flag? To fly atop the Capitol building? What they ought to put up there is a lighted sign after the Legislature goes home saying, "It's OK to come out now, they're gone."

The state flag flies over the governor's mansion, too. Is that really necessary? Why couldn't we get a flag with Governor Miller's smiling face and put it up there? No. Then Atlanta mayor Bill Campbell would want a flag with his picture on it flying over City Hall and imagine how much something that big would cost city taxpayers.

OK. So we keep a state flag, but how do we design it to keep everybody happy? How about a flag with a big peach on it? We're the Peach State, aren't we? How about a flag with Herschel Walker's picture on it? Heisman Herschel helped win a national football championship for the University of Georgia. And personally, I'm a lot more proud of that than the fact the South lost the war and its objective, making Northern men dress better when they visit our beaches. (No long black socks with sandals, you guys.)

The *Wall Street Journal* once praised local barbecue in an article leading up to the Democratic National Convention in 1988. A flag with a giant hog on it maybe? But not everybody likes barbecue. Some people in the state don't even eat meat at all. And they would be screaming for a flag with an asparagus spear or a broccoli stalk, and I'd throw up every time I saw it.

A flag to suit everybody. I'm still thinking.

I've got it. If it's a given we really need a state flag, then in order to please everybody we should fly a flag with all sorts of colors on it.

One that is red and yellow, black and white, and green for the vegetarians.

You look up at the state flag and figure out for yourself what you want it to symbolize. People in Atlanta once saw the image of Christ on a billboard advertising spaghetti.

And if the ghost of great-great-granddaddy Beauregard comes back to me and wants to know what happened to the Georgia flag, I'll just say, "Don't look at me. You're the one who lost Miami Beach to the Yankees."

Are Clinton, Gore Really Southerners?

IT HAS LONG BEEN MY CONCLUSION THAT IF YOU HAPPEN TO be a Straight Southern White Male (SSWM), as I happen to be, you're in a mess in the politically correct '90s.

Most of us are automatically branded as racist, sexist, anti-gay, and it is often said we drink beer and listen to Willie Nelson albums instead of sipping expensive wines while listening to a recording of Mozart's Opus No. 28 in G-flat out, Asia Minor. None of that is necessarily so, except for the part about the beer and our Willie Nelson albums.

Willie singing the phone book would, in fact, be a symphony, and most wines are overpriced and overrated, and who among us would remember to bring a corkscrew to a stock car race? But look at this, will you: The two highest ranking men in our government are Straight (I assume) Southern White Males. Pass the butter beans.

Two good ol' boys (a term Northerners, especially women with hyphenated last names who hate college football and pickup trucks, came up with) occupying the White House.

Jimmy Carter of Georgia lived in the White House for four years, but he picked Fritz Mondale from Minnesota as his running mate and nobody named Fritz ever once said, "I heard 'dat" — this is what we beer-swillers and politically incorrecters say instead of "I, indeed, concur."

But then I began to ask myself, do Bill Clinton and Al Gore really fit the SSWM mold?

I wrote in an earlier column how I once saw Al Gore cooking barbecue in Memphis. But how many of us SSWM's have a wife named Tipper? We marry women named Bonnie Lou, Ann Sue, Doris and Joe Betty Mavis.

Bill Clinton's wife is named Hillary. Hillary? Once Prince Charles gets rid of Princess Di, he'll probably marry somebody named Hillary.

And both these guys went to Ivy League schools. Most little boys who grow up in Arkansas, as did Bill Clinton, want to go to the University of Arkansas, wear a silly hat and scream "Pig Soooooie!" when the Razorbacks score a touchdown.

Al Gore didn't go to the University of Tennessee, either, where the mascot is a blue tic hound named Smokey and the band never stops playing "Rocky Top" from the opening kickoff to the final whistle.

What they do at Yale, where Bill Clinton went to school, is sing, "Boola, Boola," which is translated loosely into Southern as, "How 'bout them Dawgs!"

Does either one of these guys own a pickup truck and have a dog named Tater or Rattler or Biscuit Eater that crawls under the truck in order to sleep in the shade and emerges with oil on its back? Does either one of these guys know all the words to even one country music song?

Can they use their mouths to blow gnats off their face, or do they try to swat them away with their hands? Would either ask Congress to pass legislation outlawing instant grits?

Do they say "wrestling" or "rasslin"? Did they have a problem pronouncing "Shiite" during the Gulf War? Do Hillary and Tipper still fry chicken, or serve it baked under some awful sauce? Do they still cook at all? Before I make up my mind whether Bill Clinton and Al Gore are true SSWMs, I want answers to these questions.

SOUTHERN LIVING

Watching the World from My Front Porch

I'VE BEEN DOING A LOT OF SITTING ON MY FRONT PORCH lately. I do this late in the evenings after the intense summer heat has subsided.

I supposed there are two primary reasons. One is, television just gets more rotten by the day. I've got 50 channels but I still have trouble finding anything worth watching. I'm even tired of the Spice Channel. The plots simply never change.

I also come from a long line of front-porch sitters, and before air-conditioning and television, that's the way a lot of people used to spend their evenings.

I did that with my own family when I was growing up.

My grandfather and I used to count cars and listen for trains.

I've been sitting on my front porch with my dog Catfish, the black Lab. I count BMWs. He growls when Volvos come by.

I live on a nice street and I have a nice front porch. I have a swing and two rocking chairs. I sit in one of the rocking chairs.

The swing is a little hard on what is left of my rear. Where do men's butts go when they get older?

One thing I have noticed is there are a lot of other people, at least in my neighborhood, who aren't sitting inside watching television in the evenings, either. They aren't sitting on their porches, however. They are out engaging in some sort of exercise.

There aren't just joggers anymore. In fact, there seems to be fewer joggers everyday.

(I was sitting in my doctor's office a few weeks ago when a nurse looked in and said to him, "CNN is on the phone. They want to know your advice on running in the Peachtree Road Race in this hot weather. My doctor looked up and said, "Don't." A man had a heart attack and died in that race.) A lot of bicycle riders come by my house while Catfish and I are on the porch. They wear helmets and tight pants and race past in large packs. The other evening, maybe 15 came by in a blur. Three minutes later a lone cyclist raced past. He appeared to be attempting to catch up with the others.

"He reminds me of horses I tend to bet on," I said to Catfish.

I get a lot of people out walking their dogs. A man comes by walking a dog that looks like a rat. He sort of looks like a rat, too. They say people often begin resembling their pets after a time.

Catfish and I have been together for over a decade, but my ears seem to be the same length as always.

I get roller skaters. They tend to be younger than the other exercisers. A roller skater came by my house recently, going down hill at what must have been 35 miles an hour. If he had fallen, they would have had to scrape him up.

There's another group that comes by my house that is exercising in a manner to which I am not familiar. They aren't jogging, but they aren't simply strolling, either. They are walking very fast and slinging their arms back and forth.

"That's power walking," somebody told me. "It's not as hard on your knees as jogging."

It looks like prissing to me, but I'm nearly 50 and don't own a Nordic Trac.

It once was the custom to speak pleasantly to anybody who happened to come past while one was sitting on one's porch. I wondered how that would play in a large American city in the '90s.

So one night whenever the joggers, power walkers or dog walkers would come by (the roller skaters and cyclists were going too fast,) I would call out, "Good evening."

Amazing. To a person, each called back, "Good evening."

I must have said "Good Evening" twenty times, and not once did anybody ignore my attempt to be pleasant.

That made me feel awfully good. Made me feel good about myself, my neighbors and my region.

We may even take up front porch sitting full time, me and ol' Catfish. He said he thought the power walkers looked like they were prissing, too, by the way.

We don't look alike, but I guess we're starting to think alike as we enter our rocking chair years.

As 50 Looms,
There Are Still a Few Surprises

ONCE YOU BEGIN STARING AT THE HALF-CENTURY MARK AS I am, you figure it rather unlikely there are any completely new experiences left.

I'd already been to Paris and the Texas State Fair, and I played golf with Arnold Palmer once.

But.

Her mother and I have been keeping company, and when it was Daddy Day at her pre-school, Jordan picked me to go with her.

Jordan is 3 and she has blonde hair and she wore a pretty white dress and had a yellow ribbon in her hair.

We had a difficult time finding her school. Every time I would turn, following her mother's directions, Jordan would scream, "No, no, you are going the wrong way!" Here I was, a grown man trying to locate a school in rush hour traffic with what turned out to be a terrible set of directions and a 3-year-old screaming, "You're going the wrong way!" Women.

We found the school, however, and there I stood with 15 other pre-schoolers and their daddies.

The first thing we did is paint with a golf ball. I know it doesn't sound possible, but it is. What you do is take a golf ball, dip it into some green paint and then dip it into some blue paint.

Then you put the golf ball on a piece of paper in a box. You put a lid on the box, and then you shake the box and make the ball roll around inside it.

The result is a piece of paper with a lot of green and blue lines and splotches on it.

I gave Jordan the Grizzard Golf Ball Blot Test. "What does this look like to you?" I asked her, holding the piece of paper in front of her.

She pondered for a moment and then said, "Catfish."

Catfish is my dog, the black Lab. Jordan likes to pull his tail. He likes to hide from Jordan.

Actually, the green and blue lines and splotches didn't look like Catfish at all. They looked like the *USA Today* weather map gone berserk. Or like a blue-and-green Edsel. What do I know about golf-ball painting?

After that, we went to the music room. The daddies had to sit down on a rug with their children.

Each child was given a felt outline of a different farm animal. When that animal was called by the music teacher, the child with that animal went to a board and stuck his or her animal on it, and then we all made the sound that particular animal makes.

It had been a long time since I sat on a rug and did animal sounds. I oinked like a pig, barked like a dog, baaa-ed like a lamb, whinnied like a horse, meowed like a kitten and mooed when Jordan went to the board with her cow.

I was a little disappointed they didn't have a donkey,

because I do a dynamite donkey. A college roommate of mine, George Cobb, who was in West Virginia the last time I heard of him, taught me.

You whistle through your front two teeth and then go "Ha wwnk!" Well, it was fun in college when you'd had a few beers.

I made a note to teach Jordan how to do a donkey in case they get one at her school.

The last thing that happened was the children sang a song, and when they got to, "I love you," they were supposed to point to their daddies.

Jordan pointed to me.

It was, in fact, a completely new experience, and it was also the first time, I was thinking, a female had ever asked me out.

As the daddies were leaving, all the children gave their hug. Jordan put her arms around me, and I think she really enjoyed having me there.

I may have missed something in my first 45 years. I really may have missed something.

Springtime,
Flowers Seem to Grow on You

WHY IS IT THE OLDER YOU GET THE MORE YOU BEGIN TO notice things you really never paid much attention to before? Simple things. Quiet things. Natural things.

It's been that way for me, for instance, with flowers. When I was growing up in Moreland, my Aunt Jessie's yard was the flower capital of the county. People drove from as far away as Grantville, Corinth, and Smith City to gaze at the color show Aunt Jessie's yard put on each spring.

I never paid much attention to her flowers, myself. The only time I ever thought about them was when Aunt Jessie would berate me for tromping through her flowers in search of the baseball I just hit from my yard to hers.

"Get out of those flowers, young man!" she must have screamed at me a million times. I never understood her concern. There I was practicing to grow up to be Gil Hodges, and how could I continue without my baseball?

Now flowers slay me. The azaleas will be blooming in Atlanta soon. So will the dogwoods. Their beauty decorates the city in pinks and whites and takes an ol' flower stomper's breath.

This week there have been days that were certainly whispers of spring. It was warm and still and it chased away the dreariness of winter. I spent one afternoon on the golf course. On one hole, the sprinkler system was wetting the grounds around it. I smelled a smell I hadn't thought of in years. The smell of water upon dry soil.

I can't describe that smell in words, but I remembered it from when the rain used to hit the dusty dirt road in front of my grandmother's house. Also, I remembered it from when I would be in my grandfather's fields, following him as he followed his plow and his mule, and it would "come up a cloud," as the old folks used to say, and the rain pelted down upon the freshly plowed earth and produced that smell again.

I looked up at an absolutely clear, blue sky this week. Its brilliance was remarkable. Up there somewhere was a hole in the ozone layer, but I couldn't see it. All I saw was a blue so clear and so bright it was like looking into eternity.

It's also difficult to describe the feeling of warmth. It's a secure feeling, somehow. I just sort of stood out there on the golf course and wallowed in it.

When chill turns to warm, it may be whoever created all this reminding us an end does finally come to winters of discontent. This is my forty-fifth spring. But it was only the last several years that I began to take a few moments to relish them.

I vividly remember that first time I really noticed and appreciated the coming of spring. I was on a golf course then, too. Augusta National. I had just turned 30. I was covering the Masters golf tournament for the Chicago *Sun Times*.

I was standing on number 16 on an April Sunday that was spectacular. It was warm and cloudless. There was the green of the turf, the blue of the sky, the pink of the azaleas. I would be catching a flight in a few hours, back to Chicago. I'd called the office earlier. They said it was snowing.

I stood out there and soaked it all in for the first time. It did something to my soul. It also did something to my future. I vowed at that moment I'd never miss another Georgia spring.

Twenty-two days later I was back at home in Atlanta with a job as a typer of words upon blank sheets of paper.

Fifteen years later I am still taking the time to smell and feel the glory of springtime. Getting older does have its benefits.

Sorry about the flowers I stomped, Aunt Jessie. I never learned to hit a curve ball anyway.

Alcohol, Tobacco and Firearms

JUST ABOUT THE TIME WE FINALLY ARE CONVINCING THE rest of the nation that we don't do things like eat mud in the South and that we have paved roads and indoor toilet facilities, the following had to hit the news: According to newspaper reports, Georgia Department of Revenue officials say the consumption of untaxed whiskey in the state is on the rise. "Untaxed whiskey" is an Atlanta way of saying moonshine, or white lightning.

Here the state of Georgia is going to be the host of the 1996 Olympics and the Department of Revenue tells us, not to mention the rest of the nation, Pappy's back at the still cooking up a new batch of corn liquor. The department came out with its statement after a 77-year-old Morgan County man was arrested for bootlegging Mason jars filled with moonshine.

The reason given for the increasing taste for moonshine was the rise in prices of legal liquor. And what are the chances you could get your hands on a Mason jar filled with enough kick to send you to the cemetery? "Bootleggers," Georgia's chief revenue officer was quoted as saying, "are starting to pay more attention to the quality of their product. They're a lot smarter than they used to be. They don't want to kill off their customers."

One wonders if the airlines and the tobacco industry could learn from that. I come from rural Georgia and I partook of a Mason jar one night. We were all about 15. We held the jar against a light and noticed a lot of unidentifiable things floating around inside the 'shine.

"Probably just a few sticks and bugs," said my boyhood friend and idol, Weyman C. Wannamaker Jr., a great American, who proceeded to purify the liquid by straining it through his T-shirt. I was terribly ill the next morning. My mouth felt like the entire Chinese army had bivouacked in it the night before. My head felt like it had gotten into a disagreement with Mike Tyson's fists.

I never drank any more moonshine after that, and Weyman didn't either. "Dang stuff ate right through my favorite T-shirt," he said.

So we're headed back to Thunder Road, huh? Recall Robert Mitchum outrunning the revenuers in that '50s black and white classic? It wasn't that far from the truth. A Georgia mountain man once entered a stock car race at the old Lakewood Raceway in Atlanta when stock car racing was still on red dirt.

Revenuers appeared on the scene after receiving a tip his car was a tanker and loaded with white lightning. The mountain man won the race, but he never stopped to get his trophy or cash. He crossed the finish line and just kept going and escaped from the tax boys again.

But as interesting as all that is, the idea of moonshining making a comeback in Georgia is unsettling to me. We've come a long way to prove we no longer live on

Tobacco Road, or God's Little Acre.

So, as much as it goes against my raisings, I'm pulling for the revenuers this time. The Falcons are enough of an embarrassment to Atlanta and the state. We didn't need this, too.

See This Badge?
Watch Your Step in My Fife-dom

I RECENTLY PURCHASED A PARCEL OF LAND WITH A HOUSE on it on the banks of Lake Oconee in Georgia. A beautiful new golf course called Great Waters is almost at my door.

There is serenity here. I often need it. I'm only an hour and a half from Atlanta, but it's a completely different world.

I haven't heard a single siren so far, and I can watch the sun rise over the lake in the morning. There's a constant breeze off the water, and my dog Catfish, the black Lab, spends more time in the lake than out of it when we are here.

It's all got to do with getting older, I suppose, when it's lake breezes and sunrises that make me the happiest instead of being out there running where the neon can blind a man and do terrible things to his priorities.

All this to give you a sense of the place where something very extraordinary has happened to me.

This is one of those type things one never tells without first saying, "You aren't going to believe this, but. . . ." OK. You're not going to believe this, but the sheriff of Putnam County had me over to his office the other day and swore me in as a deputy. He gave me a badge. It has my name on it.

The reaction I have gotten when I mention I'm now a law officer person comes in the form of two questions: First people have asked, "Do what?" After that, they follow up with the same second question. "Did they give you a bullet?" It's the Barney Fife thing. Sheriff Andy Taylor of Mayberry would never allow his deputy, Barney, to have more than one bullet, and he made him carry it in his shirt pocket. So these individuals think they are very witty and clever when they make the references to Barney.

No, I wasn't given a bullet. I wasn't given a gun, either. I didn't want a gun. Guns frighten me. And recall that Andy Taylor didn't have a gun either. Yet he was able to maintain order in Mayberry quite well. And also recall in *Walking Tall* that Sheriff Buford Pusser cleaned up his town with a big stick, not a gun.

After the sheriff gave me my badge, I asked him where I should keep it.

"Attach it inside your wallet," he said. I did. And I've been practicing opening my wallet and flashing my badge, as in "I'm the heat, ma'am, all I want are the facts."

Joe Friday. Lewis Thursday.

I am, of course, certain the Putnam sheriff made me a deputy just for laughs, and that my position is an honorary one. But I'm proud of it, anyway. I feel like I'm a part of this area now, not just some city slicker who needs to get away from the madding crowd on occasion.

But I'm also aware of this: My position might be an honorary one, but I've still got the badge, and if you're passing through Putnam County, be careful you don't let me see you speeding, making illegal turns, or failing to slow for a yield sign.

Motorists who do such a thing and get away with it might think they can get away with other violations as well. You've got to stop small crimes before they become large ones.

Jaywalk today and commit a 117 (running naked through town) tomorrow.

You've got to nip it in the bud. Nip it, nip it, nip it.

Roots and Berries

THE WAY I FIGURE IT, YOU SPEND THE FIRST HALF OF YOUR life attempting to get away from your roots and the second half trying to get back to them.

My roots are deeply bedded in the Georgia soil. My grandfather had 12 acres of the stuff, and from it he grew countless tables full of fresh vegetables.

Perhaps what made them even better was the fact he did most of his growing from behind a mule. Tractor vegetables are OK, but mule vegetables have a more honest and genuine flavor, I think.

I was drafted at an early age to help in the activity of growing. My grandfather even allowed me to hold the plow occasionally as the mule trudged down the row.

Many times, the mule took control of me and began veering off course and ignoring my pleas of "gee" (go right) and "haw" (go left). But my grandfather was always right there to bring the mule to order.

But I did other things, such as gathering plowed-up potatoes, hoeing weeds and pulling corn.

To be honest, it didn't take long to realize agriculture wasn't in my future. It was hot, dirty, tiring work. I envisioned myself in an air-conditioned office rather than as a toiler in the fields.

So when the opportunity arose, I split. And it had been 30 years — the reign of Johnny Carson — since I had involved myself in any sort of activity that dirtied my hands.

But then, I began to notice those smells again, the smell of rain, the smell of rain upon dusty earth, even the smell of freshly plowed ground. Most of these scents came back on golf courses, oddly enough.

They began to haunt me. I even began picking up handfuls of southern soil, just to smell it and feel its wondrous texture again.

There was something missing in my life.

Get a grip.

Here's what I decided to do: Plant a garden.

Long removed from the furrowed fields of my youth, I decided to see if I could grow anything.

I had some help. Tom broke up a small plot in my urban back yard. Dedra and Jordan helped with the planting. I dug the holes with my hands and Jordan, who is nearly 4, dropped in the speckled-heart butter beans.

Tom had brought me some gloves. I refused to wear them.

"Real gardeners don't wear gloves," I said to him.

So the three of us set out butter beans, tomatoes, squash, okra, peppers, cucumbers, and watermelon, and Tom took pictures so I would have proof.

I also worked barefoot and got my feet, between my toes, and my hands marvelously dirty.

That was a week ago. I've watered and fertilized and

things do seem to be growing. Even the butter beans Jordan and I planted are meekly sprouting.

So if I can keep the bugs and the birds away, I might soon be able to sit down to a plate of food I actually grew myself. Imagine that.

The headline should read: Grizzard returns to the soil; garden said mild success.

I may even expand next year and plant the entire back yard.

Anybody know where there's a good mule for sale?

GREENS, GRITS, GRAVY AND OTHER GOOD EATIN'

Kiss My Grits

AS ONE OF THE NATION'S LEADING EXPERTS ON GRITS (MY mother served them every morning for breakfast), all I can do is try to light the way for those still blinded by prejudice and fear.

Grits won't bite you. Grits taste good and they're good for you.

Just sit back and relax and put yourself in my hands and let's go.

**GRIZZARD'S GUIDE TO A SOUTHERN DELICACY
FOR FOLKS FROM NEW JERSEY
AND PLACES LIKE THAT**

☛ *The origin of grits:* Cherokee Indians, native to the Southern region of the United States, first discovered grits trees growing wild during the 13th century. Chief Big Bear's squaw, Jemima Big Bear, is said to have been out of oatmeal one day, so she gathered the tiny grits growing from the grits trees and cooked them in water for Chief Big Bear.

After eating the grits, Chief Big Bear ordered his squaw, Jemima, burned at the stake.

Later, however, Southern planter Jim Dandy found grits taste a lot better if you put salt and pepper and butter on them. Grits really took off in the South after that. Today, grits orchards may be seen from the Carolinas to Florida and west to Louisiana.

At some orchards, tourists may "pick their own grits." If you decide to give it a try, make certain each grit you pick is ripe and firm. Raw grits tend to stick to the roof of your mouth and have been known to choke even large goats.

☛ *How grits got their name:* From the Cherokee word, *grayette,* which means "corn pebbles." The Cherokees thought grits were tiny versions of corn. They even tried to make bread from grits, which brought about another big run on squaw-burning.

☛ *What does the word "hominy" mean?* It is Southern for "blended voices," as in, "That quartet sure makes nice hominy, don't it?"

☛ *How do we prepare grits?* First, go out to your grits

trees and pick a peck of grits. Wash, then allow to soak in warm buttermilk for an hour. Add two tablespoons of Jack Daniel's (Black Label) Tennessee sippin' whiskey and one cup branch water. Stir, bake at 450° for approximately one hour. Cover with sawmill gravy, add butter, then salt and pepper to taste. Cheese (Kraft American) optional.

Must be served hot. Cold grits tend to get gummy. You wouldn't serve cold, gummy grits to Communist sympathizers from New York.

☛ *What are some other uses for grits?* Patching blowouts. Snake bites. Bathroom caulking. In some parts of the South it is even believed grits will grow hair. This is doubtful.

Grits do make a delightful party punch, however. Just add more Jack Daniel's.

☛ *How can I order my grits tree?* By sending $38.95 for each tree desired to "Grits-a-Grow-Grow," in care of Grizzard Enterprises. Add $15 if you want to take advantage of our special offer for our handy "Grit-Picker," which will save time and wear and tear on your hands when you go out to gather grits off your new grits tree.

☛ *What else may I order from "Grits-a-Grow-Grow"?* A special brochure outlining how you can purchase valuable vacation property at our new Alligator Point resort in Florida and about six zillion copies of Amy Carter's Washington Coloring Book. Order now while they last.

Verily, Putteth Not Sugar into Ye Corn Bread

I CAN PRIDE MYSELF ON TWO RECENT, MAJOR ACCOMPLISH-ments. Both have to do with my fondness for down-home Southern cooking. I favor down-home Southern cooking because I am from a down-home Southern home. That, and it tastes good.

I want my chicken fried, gravy on my steak, and I want my green beans cooked and my tomatoes served raw. Too many fancy restaurants serve their green beans raw and then they cook their tomatoes — and give you some sort of hard, dark bread with it. This is an unholy aberration I cannot abide.

I find some of the best down-home Southern cooking at the Luckie Street Grill in Atlanta, which features fried chicken, country-fried steak, meatloaf and, on Fridays, beef tips on rice and home-cooked vegetables — and uncooked tomatoes, of course. Imagine my shock, however, when I went to order my vegetables one day and the list on the menu included "Northern beans."

"There must be some mistake," I said to my favorite waitress, Jo.

"This says 'Northern beans.' How can you list Northern beans in a down-home Southern cooking place?"

"What do you call them?" asked Jo.

"White soup beans, of course," I answered.

My mother used to cook white soup beans for me.

It's a little-known fact, but when Jesus fed the masses he served white soup beans with the fish and bread. "Northern" beans aren't mentioned anywhere in the Bible.

Jo said, "I'll see what I can do."

I come in a week later and it says "White soup beans" on the Luckie Street menu. Praise Him.

That was accomplishment No. 1.

Where else I often eat is at the Ansley Golf Club in Atlanta, which has good chili.

Chili is down-home as long as you don't put mushrooms in it. They serve corn bread with the down-home chili at Ansley. The problem is, the corn bread is sweet. Corn bread is not supposed to be sweet. That's in the Bible, too. The book of Martha White, 7:11.

If you want something sweet, order the pound cake. Anybody who puts sugar in the corn bread is a heathen who doesn't love the Lord, not to mention Southeastern Conference football.

Anyway, in late December I went to Ansley and ordered the chili.

"You ought to try the corn bread," said the waiter. "The chef got tired of you complaining, so he quit putting sugar in it."

I tasted the corn bread. No sugar. I called out the chef.

"Verily," I said unto him, "it's about time you stopped making a sacrilege out of corn bread."

Accomplishment No. 2.

I feel so good about my two feats, I've got two new targets for next year.

I'm going to see if I can convince fast food places to start cutting up their own french fries instead of using frozen ones, and I'm going to see if I can help white bread make a comeback in this country.

Do not underestimate me. I'm on a mission from God.

Sweet Memories, Right Off the Vine

THANKS TO THE GENEROSITY OF A COUPLE OF FRIENDS, I scored some home-grown (vine ripe, if you please) tomatoes the other day with a street value of at least seven or eight bucks.

You can get these tomatoes only in the summertime, and if you have no garden of your own, you must have a tomato connection. The rest of the year, one must be content with those tasteless pretenders somebody grows in a hothouse somewhere. They lack the juice and the flavor of the summertime home-growns to which, I freely admit, I've become addicted.

I grew up eating home-grown tomatoes from the family garden. It was only after I became an urban creature living far from the tilled soil that I realized what a blessing they had been to me as a child and how dear they are to me now.

Mama would cook green beans with new potatoes and there would be a plate of fresh tomatoes just out of the garden. The juice from the tomatoes inevitably mixed with the green beans and even got into your corn bread. The mix was indescribably wonderful.

Of course there are other ways to eat homegrown tomatoes. I took one of my friends' offerings last week and sat down and ate it like an apple. Some of the abundant juice ran down my chin onto my shirt like it did with the tomatoes of my youth. I can still hear Mama:

"Look at your shirt, and I just took it off the line."

I get my shirts dry-cleaned now. Oh, for one more of her gentle scoldings. I also use the tomatoes to make sandwiches. Behold, the fresh home-grown tomato sandwich. First, you need white bread. Never use any sort of bread other than soft, fresh, white bread — hang the nutritional value — when constructing a tomato sandwich. To use any sort of other bread is a transgression equal to putting lights in Wrigley Field and putting mushrooms on cheeseburgers.

Cover both slices of bread with mayonnaise. Salt and pepper the slices of tomatoes and then put them between the bread. Eat quickly. The juice of the tomato slices will quickly turn the white bread into mush and you will be wearing some of your tomato sandwich.

My grandfather, Bun Word, sold some of his tomatoes on the side of the road at the little fruit and vegetable stands he ran summers in my hometown of Moreland. One day he ran out of his own tomatoes and bought some to sell off a produce truck. A couple of Atlanta tourists stopped by. The lady picked up a basket of tomatoes and asked my grandfather, "Are these home-grown?"

"Yes, ma'am," he said.

She bought a basket of the tomatoes. I said to my grandfather, "You didn't grow those tomatoes at home."

"Well," he replied, "they were grown at somebody's home."

My grandfather was a God-fearing, foot-washing Baptist, but I later learned it was not considered sinful nor unethical to put the shuck on tourists. In bigger cities they allowed liquor and strippers in various dens of iniquity. The folks in the hinterlands were just getting even.

My boyhood friend and idol, Weyman C. Wannamaker Jr., a great American, for instance, once sold cantaloupes to city folk as Exotic Moreland Yellow-meated Midget Watermelons for an obscene profit.

This is just to say be careful if you go out and try to buy home-grown tomatoes. Folks in the country still don't give the rest of us much credit for being very smart. Otherwise, we wouldn't lived crammed together like we do and spend half our day fighting traffic and eating, as some do, raw fish.

I've eaten all my tomatoes now and face a rather extensive dry-cleaning bill for the damage they did to my shirts. But it will be a pittance when I consider the ecstasy and memories they provided me.

And to think, it wasn't that long ago I felt the same way about sex.

Real Home Cooking
Doesn't Fit in a Box

FOR WEEKS I HAD BEEN SEEING A TELEVISION COMMERCIAL for this certain chain of restaurants. The commercial claimed the restaurant served home cooking, "The kind mom used to do." I'm not going to name the restaurant chain. I've already got one libel suit pending. But I will say I've spent the nearly three decades since I left the cooking mama used to do looking for something, anything, that came close to it.

I grew up at a fried chicken, pork chops, pot roast and fresh vegetable table, with corn bread or mama's homemade biscuits on the side. I must have this sort of food at least once a week or be struck by the dreaded bland-food poisoning. That's because I have to eat a lot of airline food, as well as hotel food. The airlines and hotels get together each year and plan their menus. Steak au gristle and chicken a la belch.

So I gave this chain a try. I walked into one of its restaurants and looked over the menu. There was no fried chicken or pork chops. But there was country fried steak and pot roast. I decided to go for the pot roast.

"Can I get mashed potatoes and gravy with the pot roast?" I asked the waitress.

"Sure," she answered.

The pot roast was so-so. The gravy was suspect. One bite

of the mashed potatoes, and I knew. I called the waitress back over.

"I would take it as a personal favor if you would be perfectly honest with me," I said. "These mashed potatoes came out of a box, didn't they?" The waitress dropped her eyes for a brief second. Then she looked up and said apologetically, "Yes, they are."

I hate mashed potatoes that come out of a box. When God created the mashed potato (I am certain the Bible points this out somewhere), he had no intention of anybody goofing around and coming up with mashed potatoes from a box.

He meant for real potatoes to be used. You peel them, you cut them into little pieces and put them in a pot of boiling water. You put in some salt and pepper, and then you add some butter and maybe even a little sour cream and then you beat them and stir them and you've got biblically correct mashed potatoes.

I realized the waitress didn't have anything to do with the fact that the restaurant served mashed potatoes from a box in a place that advertised mama's cooking, an affront to mothers everywhere. That was upper management's doing.

So when I paid my bill — reluctantly, due to the fact there should have been a warning on the menu that the mashed potatoes weren't really mashed potatoes — I did have a word with the assistant manager, who took my money anyway. "May the Lord forgive you, for ye know not what you do, you potato ruiner."

I think he thought I was some sort of religious nut. He was still waiting for me to hand him a pamphlet and ask him for money as I walked out the door.

Mashed potatoes from a box. That's what's wrong with this country. That, and non-alcoholic beer, instant grits, canned biscuits, soybean anything, frozen french fries, fake flowers, staged photo opportunities for politicians running for re-election, tanning salons, and I bought some Häagen Dazs vanilla ice cream at the grocery store recently, but when I went to eat it, I realized I had gotten yogurt instead.

What's real anymore? Computerized voices talk to me at the airport. I phone a friend and I talk to a machine. Musical stars are lip-syncing.

Did somebody mention silicone implants? As soon as I make the world safe from boxed mashed potatoes, I'll get around to that. It's a matter of priorities, you know.

Here's the Book on Fried Green Tomatoes

A LOT OF PEOPLE WHO SAW THE MOVIE *FRIED GREEN TOMA-toes* probably asked themselves, "What's a fried green tomato?" There wasn't any dialogue that I recall concerning fried green tomatoes in the movie — just a sign outside the Whistle Stop Cafe that advertised they were on sale inside.

The type of food the movie dealt with mostly was barbecue, and if I go any further, I'd be giving away some of the plot for those who still haven't seen this "must-see" movie.

Truthfully, I hadn't thought about fried green tomatoes in a long time till I saw the movie.

My grandmother used to serve them when I was growing up, but after I left home, I don't recall eating another one.

So I set out a month or so ago trying to find some place that still served fried green tomatoes so I could reacquaint myself with their taste.

I was in a restaurant in Jackson, Mississippi, that served fried dill pickle slices. For the record, they're a perfect munchy with a cold longneck bottle of beer.

Fried eggplant is easily located in the South. Fried okra, of course, is served in just about every place that features the meat and three.

But fried green tomatoes? I searched and searched. Nothing.

But then I had business this week in the hamlet of Social Circle, 35 miles east of Atlanta, off I-20. When lunchtime came I asked a local, "Where's the best place in town to eat lunch?"

"Try the Blue Willow Inn," I was told.

The Blue Willow Inn, on the main drag in Social Circle (do they still say "main drag"?), was inside an old plantation-style home that obviously had been renovated recently.

The deal was $6.50 for all you could eat of any and everything sitting out on a couple of large tables.

I started with the sweet potato souffle. I went to the baby lima beans from there. Then to the squash casserole, the green beans, the rice, and on to the turnip greens. My plate runneth over and I wasn't to the meats and breads yet.

I piled three pieces of fried chicken on top of that and added a piece of hot, buttered corn bread. Next to the corn bread was something I didn't recognize right away.

"This wouldn't be . . ." I said to a waitress.

"Yessir," she replied. "They're fried green tomatoes."

I wound up eating 10 slices. The sweet sourness of the green tomato — quite different from the taste of red tomatoes, with the crust on the outside — was incredibly pleasing.

I talked to the proprietor, Louis Van Dyke, who said he had been in the restaurant business nearly all his life. I asked him about the fried green tomatoes.

"I was serving them a long time before the movie came out," he said. He even brought me out a green tomato and told me he bought it in a farmers market in Forest Park. You slice 'em, batter 'em, and throw 'em in the grease. Sounds easy in case somebody wants to try it.

I am a connoisseur of authentic Southern cooking, which is getting more and more difficult to locate. If I gave ratings for Southern cooking, I'd have to give the Blue Willow my absolute highest mark — five bowls of turnip greens.

Every dish was authentic and delicious.

It's Southern Pride, Battered and Fried

MY HERO AND PROFESSIONAL ROLE MODEL, CHICAGO *Tribune's* Mike Royko, had an astounding piece recently. According to Royko, at an auto plant in Normal, Illinois, an executive asked the company that ran the plant's cafeteria to offer some more variety.

"Man cannot live by tuna patty melts alone," wrote Royko.

So the cafeteria people decided to offer some Southern cooking one day. They picked the wrong day.

The Friday before the Monday that was the holiday honoring Dr. Martin Luther King Jr.'s birthday, the cafeteria was to serve barbecue ribs, black-eyed peas, grits, and collards.

Two black employees at the plant, Royko further explained, went to see the executive and complained such a meal, just two days before Dr. King's birthday, was a stereotyping of black dining habits. They threatened a boycott of the meal. The executive, who was also black, ordered the Southern dishes be stricken from the Friday menu. Meatloaf and egg rolls were served instead.

What is astounding to me is, in our search to become politically correct and more sensitive, in this one instance at least, food became an issue. Southern food. What has come to be known as soul food. And my food, too.

I think it is very important to point out barbecue ribs, black-eyed peas, grits, and collards may, in fact, be a choice dish to many black Americans. But it also sounds pretty darn good to me, a white man.

I grew up on soul food. We just called it country cooking. My grandmother cooked it. My mother cooked it.

Friends cooked it. Still do. I might not have made it through my second heart operation if it hadn't been for the country cooking of one of the world's kindest ladies, Jackie Walburn, who delivered to me in the hospital.

And my friend Carol Dunn in Orlando has served me many an enchanting spread featuring her wonderful roast pork. My Aunt Una cooked me fried chicken, speckled-heart butterbeans, turnip greens, mashed potatoes, and creamed corn as recently as Thanksgiving eve. The creamed corn, the best I ever ate, was provided by my Aunt Jessie.

Don't tell me serving food like that is an affront to the memory of Dr. Martin Luther King Jr. What it would have been in Normal is a celebration of the sort of cooking that has been prevalent in the South, both for blacks and whites, for 200 years.

Royko asked, "Next Columbus Day would it be an insult to serve spaghetti and meatballs?" What a plate of hogwash, and I can get by with that. I have a pig valve in my own heart, and I can eat my share of barbecue ribs with anybody, black or white or whatever.

To charge stereotyping over food trivialized the King

holiday. The man didn't give his life for something like that. It's silly and it's stupid and it makes me want to throw up. Had I eaten meatloaf and egg rolls for lunch, I might.

SOUTHERN ROOTS GROW DEEP

Georgian by Birth

IF I HAD SAID TO MY MOTHER, "I DON'T THINK I'LL GO TO college," at some point during the years I lived at her house, she would have killed me.

Maybe she wouldn't have killed me, but she would have inflicted severe neck and head injuries upon me.

My mother was like a lot of baby boom parents. As soon as I reached the age where I could understand the basics of the English language, she began saying to me, "I want you to have it better than I did." Translated that meant, "If you ever say, 'I don't think I'll go to college,' I'm going to inflict serious neck and head injuries upon you."

My mother grew up red-clay poor, on her father's precious-few acres in Heard County, Georgia, the only one of 139 Georgia counties that didn't have one inch of railroad tracks.

My mother — and I have my grandmother's word on this — actually did walk three miles to school barefoot. It rarely snowed in Heard County, Georgia, which is the only thing that saved me from a complete guilt trip when my mother put the "I walked three miles, etc." line on me when I complained I didn't have a Thunderbird.

There were five children in my mother's family. The eldest, Uncle Johnny, also walked three miles to school barefoot and later became a doctor. I wish I could say he became a podiatrist but I can't. Well, I could, but I'd be lying. My mother, the third child, was the only other member of the family to get a degree.

My mother graduated from Martha Berry College in Rome, Georgia. Berry offered students from poor backgrounds one choice: Come here and wash dishes, clean toilets, work on our farm, and we'll give you an education. My mother, in other words, was never a member of a college sorority.

She finished Martha Berry in the '30s with a degree in education. Then she married my father, then World War II broke out, I was born in '46, Daddy went to Korea in 1950, came back from his second war a complete mess, and left my mother when I was six and she was forty-one.

We left Fort Benning, Georgia, my father's last station, and moved in with my mother's parents in a tiny little house in Moreland. My grandparents moved there from Heard County in the '40s when the few red-clay acres could no longer provide. My grandmother went to work in a local hospital as a maternity nurse. My grandfather got a job as janitor at the Moreland Elementary School.

Mother had never used her degree. Marriage and a child and life as a military wife had stripped her of an opportunity to do so. But it's 1953, she doesn't have a dime, her husband has just split, and no child of hers is going to walk to school barefoot. So my mother got a job teaching first grade in Senoia, Georgia, another small town near Moreland.

Her first year of teaching, she was paid $120 a month. A month.

And one day I would blow the opportunity to make as much as $125 a week selling encyclopedias for Howard (Dipstick) Barnes.

Senoia was six miles from Moreland. Mother needed a car. She bought a 1948 Chevrolet. Its body was the color of an orange Dreamsicle. The top was blue. The stuffing was coming out of the front seat upholstery. It was hard to crank on cold mornings, and it burned oil.

Mother taught one year at Senoia, and then she got a break, which she certainly deserved at that point in her life. The first-grade job came open at Moreland Elementary. Mother got the job.

The Moreland School was maybe a quarter of a mile from my grandparents' house. Most mornings I walked to school. When I asked mother if I could go barefoot, she said, "No. You might step on a rusty nail and get lockjaw."

Ever think about all the warnings your parents gave you growing up? Could stepping on a rusty nail really give you lockjaw and cause you to die a horrible death because you couldn't open your mouth to eat?

Remember, "Never drink milk with fish, it will make you sick"? How about, "No you can't have a BB gun. It will put your eye out"?

Today parents are worried about their children joining a religious cult or becoming drug dealers. When I was growing up they were worried about us putting an eye out.

My mother would teach first grade at Moreland School for twenty years before the illness that killed her forced her to take an early retirement with a pittance of a pension for her disability.

My mother's background taught her frugality. I'm convinced my mother could have solved the federal deficit problem. She simply would have said to the government, "OK, turn all your money over to me and give me the list of what you owe." She would have had us out of the hole shortly.

I cannot remember my mother ever spending a dime on herself for something she didn't desperately need. When the old Chevy finally gave out in 1955, she did buy a new car, a green Chevrolet. When the salesman said, "I can put a radio in for another twenty dollars," my mother said, "We already have a radio at home."

I can never remember her buying more than five dollars' worth of gas at a time, either. She would pull up to the pump and say each time, "Five, please." I think she was afraid if she filled up the tank and died, she would have wasted money on whatever gas remained in her car.

Mother began saving for my college education with the first paycheck she ever earned. She bought bonds. She put cash in shoe boxes and hid them in the back of her closet.

Having enough money to send me to college when the time came consumed my mother. Besides the bonds and the shoe-box cash, she kept a coin bank, bought day-old bread, sat in the dark to save on the electric bill, never had her hair done, quit smoking, and never put more than a dollar in the collection plate at church. She used simple logic for not tithing the biblical tenth: "If the Lord wanted me to tithe that much, he wouldn't have made college so expensive."

As a matter of fact my mother did have something to do with my interest in putting words on paper. My mother was on constant grammar patrol when I was growing up.

Going to school with children from poor, rural backgrounds, as I did, I often fell in with a bad grammar crowd. What follows is a glossary of the way a lot of words were misprounounced around me constantly:

"His'n" (his).

"Her'n" (hers).

"Their'n" (theirs).

"That there'n" (that one).

"You got air asack?" (Do you have a sack?).

"I ain't got nairn." (No, I'm afraid I don't).

Mother also disliked another common grammatical error of the times. Many of my friends would say, in referring to parents, "Daddy, he went to town last night," and, "Mamma, she went with him and they didn't bring us air a thang."

"There is no reason to say, 'Daddy, he,'" my mother would say. "'Daddy' is identification enough."

"Ain't," of course, was a hanging offense. You never got away with double negatives or the popular answer to, "Have you done your homework?" "Yes, I done done it."

My mother did allow, however, certain words and phrases common to Southern speech that might not be able to stand a harsh review in the strickest sense, of whether or not they were proper.

My mother had no problem with the use of the word "fixing" in place of "going to" or "it is my intention to," as in, "I'm fixing to do my homework." I still say "fixing" and anybody who doesn't like it can stay in Boston and freeze.

My mother had no problem with certain Southern expletives, such as

"Hot-aw-mighty!"

"Dang-nab-it!"

"Dad-gum-it!

"Shut yo' mouth!" (It's not "hush yo' mouth" as some up

North think).

"Lawd have mercy."

"I'll be a suck-egg mule."

My mother would not abide, however, any form of swearing.

I never would have used the following words and phrases in this book if my mother were still alive, because it might have broken her heart. But she's gone now, and I suppose I can offer up such examples of common Southern curse words:

"Shee-yet far": Southerners can probaby say "shit" better than anybody else. We give it the ol' two syllable treatment, which brings out the ambience and adds the fire to string it out even more.

"Sumbitch": Southern, of course, for "son of a bitch." However when people from the North try to say "sumbitch" it doesn't come out exactly right. I don't think Southerners actually say "sumbitch." I think it's more "suhbitch," as in, "That suhbitch can flat play a cello."

"Got-damn": You know.

"Ice": We don't say "ass" like other people do. I can't decide exactly how we say "ass," but "ice" comes close, as in, "Shee-yet far, Randy, if that got-damn suhbitch don't watch his ice, somebody's goin' to break that cello right over his got-damn head."

LEWIS GRIZZARD ON THE SOUTH

I remember the day the letter came. It said on the front of the envelope, "This is your official University of Georgia acceptance."

Mama paid for my first quarter. It was perhaps a two-hundred-dollar lick, counting books. She also gave me two hundred dollars cash from some hidden shoe box. She hugged me when I left home and said, "I've looked forward to this day for a long time. I know you will do well and don't drink."

I would do well.

One out of two's not bad.

Southern by the Grace of God

MY MOTHER WAS THE THIRD CHILD OF CHARLES BUNYON and Willie Word of Carroll County, Georgia. They named her Christine. Her two sisters, Una and Jessie, called her "Cricket." Her two brothers, Johnny and Dorsey, called her "Teenie." Nearly three decades of first-graders she taught knew her as "Miss Christine." I always called her Mama.

Mama had that thing some teachers develop, the idea that her students were her children, too. Often when I visited her in the hospital, a nurse would come into her room and introduce herself to me and say, "Your Mama taught me in the first grade."

Reading and writing are the basis of all learning. First-grade teachers teach that. Imagine being able to take a 6-year-old mind and teach it to write words and sentences and give it the precious ability to read.

As for me, Mama taught me that an education was necessary for a fuller life. She taught me an appreciation of the language. She taught a love of words, of how they should be used and how they can fill a creative soul with a passion and lead it to a life's work.

I'm proud of my Mama the teacher.

We put Mama next to her mother and father in the plot where her younger brother, Dorsey, was buried. Each headstone was etched with the name that the dead had been called by the rest of the family.

My grandmother was "Mama Willie." My grandfather was "Daddy Bun."

Uncle Dorsey's children had called him "Pop." We had decided to put "Miss Christine" on Mama's headstone. That's what her legion of first-graders called her.

It was over so quickly at the grave site. A few words. Another prayer. Then the funeral people ushered the family away. To spare them from the covering of the grave, I suppose.

I greeted friends. My first ex-wife came up. We embraced. I recalled the feel of her in an instant.

We went back to the house. I wasn't planning to stay that night, either. Home was where Mama was, and she wasn't there anymore. I said my goodbyes. My girlfriend and I got into my car. I said, "Let's ride over to the cemetery before we start home."

There were still a lot of flowers. The red clay over Mama's grave was moist. A man I didn't know drove up in a truck. He was an older man. He wore overalls.

"I'm the one what dug the grave," he said to me. "I had to figure out a way not to dig up any of your boxwoods in your plot. I just came back to see the pretty flowers."

The gravedigger. I was talking to Mama's gravedigger, and the man had gone to extra trouble for a family he really didn't know. I thanked him. Only in a small town.

We drove away. Moreland was behind us in a matter of

minutes. I began to hum "It Is No Secret."

My girlfriend touched my shoulder. Mama had touched my soul.

A Farewell Salute to Sergeant Dews

Several years ago, I wrote a book about my father, a veteran of World War II and Korea, who died in 1970.

Captain Lewis M. Grizzard Sr. was a highly decorated soldier, but after he returned from Korea — where he had survived a bloody rout of his company by the Chinese and had survived only because a young Chinese soldier, attempting to surrender to the Americans, had hidden him from the enemy in a cave for six weeks — he was a changed man.

He began to bender-drink heavily. He couldn't handle the family finances and borrowed large sums of money. He eventually left the army, or the army left him.

My mother could no longer cope with my father's problems and had a 6-year-old on her hands. She moved us to her parents' home and eventually divorced my father.

I wasn't certain I could write the book. I didn't know if there was enough there. And there was so much about my father I didn't know.

He roamed the country from 1954 until his death. He taught school, sold shirts, ran restaurants, and the drinking just got worse. It was a stroke that killed him.

In order to write the book, I felt I needed to know more about Korea, the forgotten war. So I bought an oral history of Korea as told by those Americans who were there.

It was a huge volume. I took it off a shelf at the bookstore and opened it to the middle.

The first name I saw was that of Sergeant Robert Dews. Bobby Dews had been my father's first sergeant when he returned from Korea and was stationed at Fort Benning.

My dad's new assignment after Korea had been to run the athletic program at Benning. Bobby Dews also played baseball for him.

I would hear daddy speak of his talent and friendship on many occasions.

The sergeant noticed a byline of mine when I was with the Atlanta *Journal* sports department 20 years ago. I went by Lewis Grizzard Jr. back then. He wrote me a letter. He told me of his connection to Daddy and that he knew of his recent death.

He also wrote, "No matter what happened to the captain after Korea, never judge him too harshly. He had been through two wars and had seen so much blood, gore and death. It haunted him and the only way he could forget for a time, was by drinking.

"I sat by him at his desk at Benning and saw his hands shake. Many times, I'd say 'Captain, let's go for a ride and get you out of here.' But he'd always go back to the bottle. I wish I could have done more for him."

I knew there was something providential about opening that huge book to a page where Sergeant Dews' name appeared, so I began my own book.

During the writing I said a lot of things and felt a lot of things I needed to say and feel.

They buried Robert P. Dews the other day in Americus. He was 77.

He had a minor league baseball career after he left the army. His son, Bobby, followed. He later was the Braves' minor league field coordinator.

I learned of the sergeant's death too late to make the funeral. But I did want to write something in his honor. Something that could never square my father's debt to him but something that would say a little boy who used to sit on the bench next to his Daddy during Ft. Benning baseball games is thankful for what he tried to do for his Daddy.

I guess Sergeant Dews was Captain Grizzard's best friend. The preachers say we'll all be reunited.

Oh, let it be so.

First Cousins Made Lasting Impression

I'VE WRITTEN QUITE A LOT ABOUT MY PARENTS, GRANDPAR-
ents and aunts and uncles. But I've never had much to say
about my cousins, and I'll limit this to first cousins for
brevity's sake.

I'm not certain how many living first cousins I have. My
parents divorced when I was young, and you lose touch.
But I can still come up with enough to fill a twin-engine
charter flight, and I thought I would offer a list and
describe a bit about each one. Some had a profound impact
on my life.

Gwen: Once lined me up with a couple of her lovely
friends. I didn't marry either of them, however. Nor did I
marry any of my cousins. Cousin-marrying went out in the
South after the birth of whoever it was who invented
instant grits.

Albert: He and I are left to carry on the Grizzard name.
He has daughters. I have no children, but plenty of time left
on my biological clock. Right?

Melba: She's the only one of my cousins who is younger
than me. We grew up together in our hometown of Moreland. One day when we were barely out of diapers, a bull
got out of its pen and began to chase us.

"Run for it, Melba!" I screamed.

Melba picked up a rock and hit the bull between the eyes

with it and it ran away. Melba saved my life. As far as I know, however, Melba never made it to Pamplona. Good news for the bulls there.

Mary Ann: Melba's sister. She was very smart and married the smartest boy in Moreland. They had lots of smart children. Now they also have lots of smart grandchildren. We're getting old, Mary Ann. Seems like only yesterday you were quashing the Santa Claus myth for us younger kids.

Lynn: She's where my looks went.

Jim: Lynn's handsome brother. A nearby women's college named Jim the best looking man at the University of Georgia when he was a student there and invited him to a banquet in his honor. Legend has it, he wore white socks with his tuxedo to the banquet. Jim never married until he was in his late 40s. He's another one of my smart cousins.

Gerry: She babysat me when I was a child. If sweet and kind had faces, they would have hers. She taught me to play Monopoly, but where was she when I invested in all those limited partnerships?

Glenda: Gerry's sister. We were inside Cureton and Cole's store in Moreland one day when I was 8. Glenda was 12. There were some grapes sitting on a counter. "Like grapes?" Glenda asked me. "Love 'em," I answered.

"Why don't you take one?" she suggested. "They won't mind."

I pulled off one and ate it.

"You know you're going to hell for stealing that grape,"

Glenda said. That was the last thing I ever stole.

Scooter: Gerry and Glenda's brother. Great fisherman, great hunter and former county drag racing champion. He taught me to throw a curve ball. They hated the dreaded hook in Region 2-AA in '63 and '64.

Mickey: She also babysat me as a child and is why I've always had a thing for redheads, which, incidentally, has cost me about as much as those limited partnerships.

Mary Jean: The classiest lady I've ever known. She wouldn't serve instant grits to a liberal Yankee Democrat.

It should be obvious I've been blessed with some great cousins. And if we had a family business, I wouldn't hesitate to put a single one of them in charge of it.

Great Memories of a Grandfather Go Pedaling Past

I WAS THINKING ABOUT MY BICYCLE. IT WAS RED. WHEN I rode it, down a thousand dirt roads with no names and even five miles to Raymond Lake, I was the wind. Or at least a large Greyhound bus.

A couple of things prompted such thoughts. One is that bicycling has become an adult thing now. Grown people pedal by my house on a regular basis. They have bicycles that appear to be very expensive.

They also wear helmets and tight-fitting cyclists' outfits. A uniform wasn't necessary during my bicycle period.

I got my red bicycle when I was 9, thanks to my grandfather, Bun Word. My grandfather was a janitor at my elementary school. A kid today probably would be embarrassed if his grandfather was the janitor at his school. I wasn't. My grandfather was in his 60s when I was 9 and in the fourth grade. But he was still a tall, muscular man that dogs followed.

He told silly jokes to my classmates and passed out an occasional stick of gum with the warning, "Don't chew it until school's out."

Some heeded the warning; most didn't. My grandfather also farmed 12 acres and helped out over at the Atlanta and West Point railroad depot, and his days were full, up to an April afternoon 30 years ago when we found him slumped behind his tractor, holding his chest. He died a week later.

My grandfather got up at 5:00 each morning and walked in the cold and dark to school. Each room was heated by a coal-burning stove.

He would go down in the coal bin under the school and haul up the coal for the fires in a wheelbarrow. When we arrived three hours later, our rooms would be toasty and comfortable.

In the afternoon, he would return to the school and clean the wooden floors and throw out the trash. That's how I got my bicycle. We all used Blue Horse paper and notebooks. Each Blue Horse product had a label with a point value on it. The more expensive the product, the more points the label was worth.

You could save Blue Horse labels and when you got enough points you could send them in and Blue Horse would send you back a prize. If you saved 25,000 points, you got the grand prize, a bicycle.

Most of my classmates didn't save Blue Horse points. They threw their labels into the trash and my grandfather would go through each wastebasket and pick out the labels.

He started saving Blue Horse points when I was 7. Two years later, he counted one day, and he had 25,000 points.

We bundled the labels together with rubber bands and mailed them to Atlanta. Two weeks later my red bicycle came.

My grandfather held on to the back of the bicycle until

I learned to ride it without adult assistance. It was a big day in my life.

I rode my bicycle until I was 14. Then it wasn't cool to ride a bicycle anymore, so one day I climbed down off it for good, counting the days until I could get my driver's license.

It is very unlikely I will take up adult cycling.

But as they pedal by my house, the memory of a precious old man comes back and touches me at midlife when I find myself looking back more often than I look ahead.

Landing in Maturity's Speed Trap

DUDLEY STAMPS AND I HAVE BEEN FRIENDS SINCE THE second grade in Moreland.

In baseball, Dudley caught and I pitched. If there had been anybody around to scream, "You da man!" in baseball games back then, that person would have screamed it when Dudley launched another home run. He hit five in one game.

Dudley was a legend by the time he was 12. He started shaving when he was 9, and in the eighth grade he fought the school bully, Frankie Garfield — who was two years his elder — to a draw. It was a moral victory for us wimps that Frankie had had many a field day picking on.

As Dudley got older, he developed a great interest in seeing how fast he could drive a motorized vehicle. When he turned 16, his parents lost their minds and gave him an earlier model Thunderbird. The rest is speeding-ticket history. Parents warned their children: Don't get in a car with Dudley Stamps.

After a high school baseball game one evening in the county seat of Newnan, I didn't have a ride home so Dudley gave me one back to Moreland, six miles away. Dudley could do Newnan to Moreland in about 200 telephone poles an hour.

The road curved for the first four miles, so Dudley had to keep it in the high double digits. Then, however, came the Moreland Straight, a flat stretch of two miles that was Dudley's Bonneville Salt Flats.

When we hit the Straight, Dudley floored it. The state patrolman who pulled him over just outside the Moreland city limit sign said, "Son, did you know you were going 108 miles an hour?"

"No I wasn't," protested Dudley. "I top-ended at 127."

A charge of merely going 108 in a 60 mph speed zone was an affront to the streak of lightning we knew as Dudley.

I begged Dudley to slow down that night. I equated speed, and still do, with death. But Dudley just laughed at me and stepped down even harder on the accelerator.

So I'll keep this short: I played golf with Dudley recently at Orchard Hills Golf Club (a.k.a. Moreland National), which sits a wedge shot from the Moreland Straight. We hit our shots on a downhill par 3. I was driving the golf cart.

There was a sign near the cart path that read: Slow, steep grade. But I'm a bat-out-of-hell's-bunker in a golf cart. Full bore, we tooled down the steep grade.

Dudley screamed, "Slow down! You're going to turn this thing over!" I hit the brakes and savored the moment. I had tugged on Superman's cape. I had taken the mask off the Lone Ranger.

I had frightened Dudley Stamps in a motorized vehicle. Thirty years later I had my revenge.

I am a blur my very own self. I am the wind.

"You're a damned fool driving a golf cart like this," Dudley, slowed by maturity, had said.

Now, come out, Frankie Garfield, wherever you are.

Me and My Guccis

ALL MY ADULT LIFE, I HAVE ATTEMPTED TO RISE ABOVE MY humble beginnings. Take shoes, for example. Now that I have steady work and live in the city, I like to wear nice shoes.

In the boondocks, we didn't wear shoes unless it was an absolutely necessity. Like your feet would freeze if you didn't, or there was a funeral.

My boyhood friend and idol, Weyman C. Wannamaker Jr., a great American, didn't wear shoes even on those occasions, but he did wash his feet twice a week whether they needed it or not.

The first time I saw Weyman in a pair of shoes, they were forced upon him. We were in the sixth grade, and the teacher organized a field trip to Atlanta to hear a performance by the symphony orchestra. As the bus pulled away from the school, she noticed Weyman was barefooted.

Horrified, she ordered the bus driver to stop at the nearest shoe store, where she bought Weyman a pair of shoes. He protested, but the teacher hit him in the mouth, and Weyman didn't mention the shoes again.

During the performance of the symphony orchestra, however, Weyman's feet began hurting him, so he took off his shoes and hung his bare feet over the railing of the balcony. Unfortunately, he was between washes.

The entire percussion section and two flute players

stopped in the middle of Chopin's Movement No. 5 to search for what had obviously passed away days earlier.

I always think of Weyman when I pull on a new pair of shoes. Lately, some of the fellows down at the lodge have been giving me the business because I now own a pair of stylish loafers by Gucci, the famous Italian leatherperson.

I prefer to think their boorish, catty remarks stem from ignorance, sprinkled with at least a tad of jealousy.

The other day, I called Weyman C. Wannamaker Jr. back home and told him I am now wearing Guccis. I knew he would be proud.

"You wearing them shoes," he said, "is like putting perfume on a hog."

FAITH IN THE BIBLE BELT

Gimmee That Old Time Religion

I GREW UP HEARING THAT GOOD THINGS COME TO THOSE who love the Lord; the Moreland, Georgia, Methodist Church was deeply and comfortably seated in the traditional interpretation of the Word. But religion, like so many other things, isn't as simple as it used to be. Nowadays the good guys sometimes wear black and white striped hats instead of just one or the other.

Almost every day in the mail I receive a letter from some television evangelist asking me for a donation to help buy a new truck for his television equipment or to pay off the debt for the new gym at New Testament University. The implication is that if I don't send them cash, I'm on the express train for hell.

Will I end up down there with Hitler and Attila the

Hun and Bonnie and Clyde just because I didn't send them five bucks for a new wrestling mat? Then again, is hell actually *down* there?

"Can you dig your way to hell?" I asked the preacher when I was a kid.

"Guess you can," he said, "but I can tell you how to get there a lot quicker."

My grandfather wouldn't have cared much for today's bigtime television preachers. In his oft-stated opinion, preachers were supposed to marry folks, preach funerals, mow the grass around the church and administer to the needs of his flock, which meant consoling the poor soul who lost his job, whose wife ran off, and whose trailer burned to the ground . . . all in the same week.

Our preacher even used to knock down the dirt dobbers' nests in the windows of the sanctuary so the inhabitants wouldn't bother the worshippers while we was trying to run the devil out of town on Sunday morning.

Do you suppose Oral Roberts or Jerry Falwell ever knocked down dirt dobbers' nests?

My grandfather also didn't like it when younger preachers used note cards to deliver their sermons. "They ought to get it straight from the Lord," he said many a time. "Politicians use notes."

The preacher at Moreland Methodist when I was growing up suited my grandfather just fine. He drove an old car. He had only one suit. He did the yard work, didn't use note cards and always attempted to answer the questions of a twelve-year-old boy when things didn't add up. Once he even preached a funeral for a dog because that little boy, who loved the dog very much, asked him to.

What would Pat Robertson say over a dog?

What bothers me today is that for every glamour boy of the pulpit, there are thousands out there who tackle the devil daily, one on one, with little or no audience, against long odds, and, occasionally, on an empty stomach.

God bless them. And God, please don't let my grandfather — I know he's around there somewhere — find out that we've got preachers down here today who use cue cards and hang out with politicians.

"Jesus of Pasta"
Is Just a Little Hard to Swallow

Jesus in the spaghetti. It was all over the news.

There's a billboard in suburban Atlanta with a picture of spaghetti on it, and people drove by and swore they saw Jesus in there amongst the noodles.

"I still don't see it, Harold," a wife said to her husband who brought her to see the Shroud of Pasta.

"Look right there in that big glob of sauce, Loreena. It's Hee-um."

No way. I'm not going for the Jesus in the spaghetti thing.

In the first place, who knows what Jesus really looks like? Until Jesus shows up on "Donahue" or "Oprah," we won't have a clue concerning his actual appearance.

I saw the spaghetti billboard on television. I looked at it, but I didn't see Jesus, unless Jesus looks a lot like Bjorn Borg, who I thought I saw in the spaghetti.

In the second place, if Jesus decided to come back for a little visit, I just can't see God dispatching him to appear on a picture of spaghetti located outside Atlanta, Georgia. Can you?

GOD: "Son, I have a little assignment for you."

JESUS: "What's that, Dad?"

GOD: "I want you to go down just outside Atlanta, Georgia, and hide in a picture on some spaghetti on a billboard."

JESUS: "Is this the Big One? Am I supposed to judge the quick and the dead?"

GOD: "No, that's later, son. Just go down and hide in the spaghetti and see if anybody notices you."

The thing about visions is that they can be misinterpreted. My grandfather used to tell of an old farmer from his boyhood days.

One morning in church the farmer got up and said, "I've been called to preach, and I'd like to deliver the sermon this morning."

That's serious stuff, being called to preach. So the pastor invited the farmer up to the pulpit to give the message.

My grandfather recalled the farmer was the worst preacher he'd ever heard. After the service somebody went up to the farmer and asked, "How'd you get the call?"

"I walked outside the other morning and there were words written in the sky that said, 'Go preach the gospel,'" he answered.

"I saw the same thing," said the man, "but you didn't read it right. It said, 'Go plow your corn.'"

Another thing about visions and the like is if you really want to see one, you can. I was staying at a beachfront condo once and a buddy and I played a trick on another friend one evening.

He said to me, "Do you see that red light way out in the distance? Wonder if it's a boat?" There was no red light, but I went along with the story.

"I've never seen anything quite that bright a red in the ocean at night. I'm not sure what it is." Our friend said, "What are you looking at?" We answered, "That bright, red light off in the distance."

"I don't see any light," said our buddy. "I see it," I said to my co-conspirator. "So do I," he answered.

After staring out to sea for a few moments our buddy finally said, "OK, now I see it. That bright, red light. Probably a fishing boat or the Coast Guard."

The same thing has happened with the spaghetti billboard, I am certain. Harold saw Jesus in the spaghetti and was able to convince his wife, Loreena, she saw the same thing. The fact that Harold earlier had stopped off for a six-pack may have helped him see it, too.

There was a great letter to the editor in the papers about all this. I paraphrase it: "Jesus might be a lot of places," said the writer, "but he's not in spaghetti." Verily.

It Pays to Listen to Voice from Above

THE *HERALD-JOURNAL* OF GREENE COUNTY, AN HOUR-and-a-half drive out Interstate 20 from Atlanta, recently carried what I consider to be one of the all-time news stories. Maybe THE all-time news story.

Keep in mind, the *Herald-Journal* is no *National Enquirer*. It doesn't carry stories about Hitler being alive and well on Neptune or stories about a woman giving birth to a duck, although the story I referred to earlier, to me, is even a bigger eye-popper.

I'll give the article's headline first: "The Lord Speaks to Pep Stone Warning Him Not to Go to Hay Field Where Over $30,000 in Machinery was Stolen in the Early Morning."

Long headline, I realize, but the reader got all the facts in a hurry.

Local citizen Pep Stone, the article stated, has been in the hay business in Greene County since 1948.

He awakened one recent morning at two o'clock. It was raining. Pep Stone had a hayfield he hadn't covered the day before.

He decided he'd better go to the field and cover it. The article quoted Pep: "I was still in bed, fixing to put on my overalls, when a voice came to me and said, 'Don't go, you will get hurt.'" Pep went back to bed. When he awakened again, he and a friend drove to the hayfield 10 miles away.

At the gate they found the lock had been shot away.

"My eyes got big and my heart skipped fast when I realized that someone had stolen my tractor and hay baler. I had paid $30,000 for this equipment," Pep was quoted further.

Tough break, but Pep put it all in perspective.

"I am living today," he said, "because of my religious belief. It was a voice that spoke loud and clear. I honestly believe if I had gone down to the hayfield, I would have been killed. I can buy some more equipment," he went on, "but I can't replace my life."

A friend who knows Pep well told me, "Pep's in church every time the door opens. If he says the Lord spoke to him, I'm not going to doubt it one bit."

Obviously the *Herald-Journal* didn't, either. Refer to the headline and realize it didn't say, "Pep Stone says the Lord Spoke to Him. . . ."

It said, "The Lord Speaks to Pep Stone. . . ."

There is a huge difference.

Most newspapers would have used the first headline, casting some degree of doubt of the Lord's personal warning. Did the Lord actually speak to Pep or did Pep just say the Lord did? Not the *Herald-Journal.* It took Pep's word and told us in something close to 36-point type that the Lord did indeed get in touch with a Greene County man and save the man from harm's way, and that's what I call a major league news story.

Do you realize the news of the Lord speaking to a mortal is bigger than news that Hitler is alive and well, a woman has given birth to a duck or that Elvis is running a car wash on the outskirts of Little Rock? Of course it is. It says to atheists they'd better make an immediate turnaround. It says maybe Jimmy Swaggart wasn't just making all that stuff up about his conversation with the Lord.

It says a marquee in front of a local church I rode past was absolutely correct: "Draw nigh with God and God will draw nigh with you." It also says there's a small town out there with a newspaper that has cast away the cynical nature of most other newspapers so that if a God-fearing local citizen says the Lord spoke to him, who is the local newspaper to cast any doubt as to the veracity of his words? Most other newspapers could use a little of that, too. Verily, verily, double-verily.

Old-Time Religion
Is Good Enough for Me

I'M LOOKING FOR THE REV. FLOYD TENNEY. HE'S THE PASTOR of a Methodist church somewhere in the Atlanta area. Somebody told me that recently, but they didn't have a name or address of the church.

I knew Floyd Tenney when I was a boy. He was a young preacher at my home church, Moreland Methodist. He was the first preacher with whom I really identified. He wasn't a somber old man in a blue suit, preaching out of Revelation, scaring me about the moon turning to blood and the seas boiling over.

The Rev. Tenney kept it simple, kept it where a young boy could get some idea of what the Methodist gospel was all about, kept it where you didn't doze off. I recall he always asked us to stand when he read from the Bible. I'd never known a preacher to ask that before.

Floyd Tenney married me for the first time in 1966 at the Moreland Methodist Church. She and I had loved each other since the sixth grade, and it was supposed to be forever.

When it turned out to be for four years, I tried to find the Rev. Tenney to help me figure out a way to get her back. But he was no longer at Moreland Methodist Church. I found out he'd gone into the used-car business. My barber died the same week I got the news about the Rev. Tenney.

My preacher goes into used cars and my barber dies in the same week. I was a lost soul. But youth gets over setbacks as it gets over almost any malady.

I found myself, moved on, and except for the mention that the Rev. Tenney was back in the pulpit somewhere, he hadn't crossed my mind in years until I attended a fancy, big-city Methodist service Sunday.

The people were nice. The minister gave a thought-provoking sermon on repentance. But they spent at least ten minutes lighting candles. The choir was in fancy robes and sang something that could have been opera. And there were all sorts of associate ministers involved, and I never heard any of the four or five hymns we used to sing.

We were asked to sing the first and third verses of some ponderous Christmas hymn with which I was not familiar. And across from it in the hymn book was "Away in a Manger." I still know all the words to "Away in a Manger," but we didn't sing that.

Concerned about this, I turned to the hymnal's index. I did find "The Old Rugged Cross" but "Precious Memories" wasn't in there.

Yes, give me that old-time religion. Give it to me as I had it when I was a boy.

The choir in Moreland Methodist occasionally was off-key, and it didn't have any fancy robes, but when they rendered "What a Friend We Have in Jesus," it was a thing of beauty and a joy forever.

When they asked Fox Covin or Western Tidwell or Clyde Elrod to pray, there were no fancy words, no quoting of big-name theologians. It just came from the heart and said, "Lord, help us to do what's right."

I've just got the feeling Floyd Tenney's church, wherever it might be in this city, is still like that. Floyd, I want to come hear you again. I want to sing the old songs.

"Would that you stand as we read God's word," you used to say.

I'll stand again as I did when I was 14, next to my mother as you read the Scriptures.

I want to sing "Precious Memories" and "When the Roll is Called Up Yonder" from that old brown Cokesbury hymnal.

It took a visit to a big-city church to make me remember how good it used to feel on the square at Moreland Methodist, where I married the first time, where I said goodbye to my mother and where they will say goodbye to me one day.

POSSUMS, COONS, GNATS AND TICKS— A SOUTHERN BESTIARY

And Other Creatures, Great and Small

The Fourth Annual Gnat Days are under way in the hamlet of Camilla located about as far south as you can go in Georgia and still not be in the bordering state of Florida, where the Northern tourist ("That's not the way we did it back in Buffalo") is the leading pest.

Camilla is inhabited by 5,400 citizens and about 8 zillion gnats, known locally as the town birds. The loose sandy soil down there is given as the reason for the abundance of the creatures.

Gnats don't bite but they get in your eyes and your ears and in your mouth if you open it to say more than three words.

Gnats also get all over your food if you try to eat out of doors. I once played in a tennis tournament known as the "Thrilla in Camilla," back before my right arm fell off and I had to give up tennis.

After my match, I was hungry. Somebody was grilling hamburgers. I got one.

Before I could take a bite, a Camillian asked me, "Why is your forehand so atrocious?" I answered, "Who wants to know, Gnatface?" which is more than three words. Seventeen hundred or so gnats flew into my mouth, and when I looked down at my hamburger, it was alive with the little black boogers.

"Go ahead and eat it," said another Camillian. "Gnat-burgers are a local delicacy."

I spit out the 1,700 or so gnats already in my mouth and gave my gnatburger to a dog who carried it off somewhere either to eat it, bury it, or have it sprayed by Orkin.

Gnat Days in Camilla is an effort to do something positive about a negative situation.

Gnat Days also include the Gnat 5K Run, an art show, and a cruise down the Flint River with the Gnat Patrol. You can buy a T-shirt with the picture of a gnat on it for $11.

What Gnat Days doesn't include is an answer to the annoying gnat question of all times: Why does "gnat" start with a "g"? I know why "gnawing" starts with a "g." If it didn't, people would get "gnawing" confused with "nawing," which is Southern for spending a leisurely afternoon saying "naw," the Southern pronunciation of the word "no."

But "nat" couldn't be confused with anything else. The Southern version of the word "evening" is pronounced "e'nin," as in, "Good e'nin, ladies."

So why did "nat" come out "g-nat"? I went to the history books to find out.

Spanish explorer Bubba DeJesus discovered South Georgia in the 1500s. While near the very spot where Camilla now stands, he became the first visitor from the Old World to encounter the gnat.

He opened his mouth to say, "Jesus! Lookito, los negros bugisimos," Spanish for "Help! I'm being attacked by 'nats,'" the Spanish word for "little bitty black bugs."

Seventeen hundred or so flew into his mouth and another covey got into his eyes. When he tried to write of his experiences in his journal, he was choking on the nats in his mouth and he couldn't see for the nats in his eyes, so he mistakenly put a "g" in front of "nats."

Unfortunately, Bubba DeJesus was run over and killed by an elderly Northern tourist driving a Cadillac soon after subsequently discovering PepsiCola, Florida, which he also misspelled in his journal as Pensacola.

He was not around, therefore, to explain why he had put the "g" in front of "nat," and the spelling stuck.

I wish Camilla great success with Gnat Days. Will I attend? Naw. Too many nats.

The Life You Save
May Be a Possum's

You walk around in San Francisco and on every corner of every street, it seems, there is somebody with a hand out asking for money to save something.

They're big on saving the rain forests out here.

"Give to save the rain forest," a guy, who looked a little like the spotted owl somebody else is trying to save, asked.

"I gave at the last corner," I said.

"I don't give a hoot," he replied, "You should give at my corner, too. If we don't save the rain forest, there won't be any more oxygen to breathe."

"Well," I said, walking away by that time, "the hole in the ozone layer will have gotten a lot bigger and we'll all be french-fried anyway."

So I saved a little on that corner, but I got hit on the next one from somebody trying to save the whales.

They're trying to save the rain forests, the spotted owl, the whales, the manatees in Florida, and whatever happened to the snail darter? After experiencing this all day, I began to wonder if I were active enough in this area and was there anything I should get behind and try to save.

Just like that, it came to me: I think I ought to get busy and try to save the possum.

What, you might be asking, do I want to save the possum from? From getting run over by some sort of motorized vehicle every time one tries to cross the road, that's what.

I don't have any research statistics to back this up, but I will be willing to bet at least eight out of every ten possums that try to get from one side of the road to the other get smushed by a car, a Greyhound bus, or a pulpwood truck.

I'm not certain how many dead possums I have seen lying smushed in the road in my lifetime's travels around the South, but I'm certain I've seen more possums than dogs or chickens, legendary road-crossers themselves.

When I was a child, in order to keep me quiet in the car, my family would count dead dogs and dead possums on the road. My grandfather would take dead dogs and I would take dead possums and every time we arrived at our destination I had always counted more dead possums than my grandfather had counted dead dogs.

Chickens and dogs, of course, cross the road to get to the other side. Why possums cross the road remains a mystery. Perhaps they are looking for other possums; I'm not Marlin Perkins here.

Whatever, it is up to us to try to save as many possums crossing the road as possible. Some may be saying, "Isn't it supposed to be 'O'- possum? That is correct, and the way possums got that 'O' in front of their names is from crossing the road and seeing headlights and thinking, " 'O' hell, I'm a goner now."

How to save the possum: Put up signs on roads that read, "Watch out for crossing possums."

Increase possum awareness so that motorists will be more sensitive and brake when they see one crossing the road.

In places where there is a high concentration of possums trying to cross the road, possum patrol persons would stop traffic in order to allow the possum to cross in safety.

Save the possum. The 'O' stands for "'O'nly You can Stop the Road Killings."

And watch for me with my hand out at a street corner near you.

Eternally Grateful
for Pigs' Sacrifice

I READ AN ARTICLE NOT LONG AGO ABOUT POLICE IN ST. Petersburg, Florida, using a pig to sniff out drugs and other contraband.

The pig did terrifically, the article said, but that didn't save the pig's job. It was dismissed from duty because it emitted an odor unpleasant to some at the station house. I ask you a question: Didn't they know ahead of time that pigs just naturally come with a pungent aroma? I've been around a few pigs in my day and, although I also found their smell less than pleasing, I understood and accepted the fact that pigs aren't supposed to smell like petunias.

Pigs rarely get a break. When one person wants to insult another, that person often mentions the pig in a disparaging way. There are many examples: "Clean up your room, Ramona. It looks like a pig sty in here."

"Harold you're disgusting. You've gotten fat as a pig."

"Who was the sweathog I saw you with last night at the Moose Club?"

I recall telling a friend that my wife had given me my first pair of Gucci shoes. "What?" he asked. "That's like putting earrings on a hog."

Well, let me say this: Since March of 1982 I've been part pig. That's when I received my first porcine aortic valve. In 1985 I got my second pig valve. That's 11 years and two pigs, both of whom gave the supreme sacrifice to help me stay alive, and I want to take this opportunity to salute them and all pigs.

Pigs are smarter than most people might think. My grandfather had three pigs named Hilda, Margaret and Big Boy. All three of them knew their names and would run to my grandfather whenever he called them.

My grandfather grew so close to his three pigs that when hog-killing time came, he didn't want to part with any of his pigs.

My grandmother said, "How can a grown man become attached to three hogs?" A compromise was made and only Hilda wound up in the freezer locker. She was older than both Margaret and Big Boy. My grandfather figured she had had about all the enjoyment a hog could have and wanted Margaret and Big Boy to get that chance, too.

My mother said when she was growing up there was a boy in her class who rode a pig to school every day.

"That pig stood out in the schoolyard and waited for him all day," she explained. "And when school was over, the boy would come out and ride his pig home again."

"One day," mother went on, "the boy showed up at school and his pig had a wooden leg."

Somebody asked, "Why has your pig got a wooden leg?"

The boy replied, "You don't eat a pig like this all at once."

(I realize there are those who know this is a stolen punch

line from another pig story, but don't spoil everybody else's fun.) For my upcoming heart surgery I'm getting a new valve. This time it will be of a mechanical sort. It's too complicated to explain why I'm not getting another pig valve; just know I'm frankly happy no other pigs will have to give up their hearts to save mine.

I want to say it's been an honor and a privilege to be part pig these last 11 years, and my eyes will always tear when I pass a barbecue joint.

I also want to thank my Nashville friend and songwriter Dick Feller for writing and dedicating a pig song to me. It's titled "Pig Polo." I think I sniff a hit.

MAN'S BEST FRIEND—NO IFS, ANDS, OR BUTS

What Evil Lurks? Catfish Knows

IT WAS A NIGHT OF TERROR I SHALL NOT SOON FORGET.

I was sitting on my living room sofa around half past eleven eating a bowl of ice cream and searching for a movie on the cable.

My dog, Catfish, the black Lab, was lying at my feet. Suddenly he arose and broke into a series of yelps.

Catfish's yelps are capable of awakening the dead.

"Timmy's not in the well again, is he, boy?" I asked.

By this time Catfish had bolted to the back door. He was clawing at it in a fever I'd never seen before in this normally placid animal.

My God, what was out there? Had Charles Manson escaped? Was it a group of liberal Democrats coming to set fire to my house? The dog was bonkers.

I certainly wasn't going to go out in the darkness of my back yard to see what lurked there and had Catfish in a frenzy.

I opened the back door and Catfish made the fastest move I'd ever seen him make.

The only other time I'd seen him leap with anywhere near the same resolve was at a pork chop that fell off my plate during a barbecuing exercise one evening.

It began a heartbeat later.

Catfish bellowed even louder. My first thought was if it's Charles Manson, he had it coming. My second thought was, if it's liberal Democrats, I've got my own personal pit bull here and didn't need Pat Buchanan.

My third thought was, Catfish has now awakened the entire neighborhood, but what could I do? Next, there came out of the dark pit that was my back yard a blood-curdling shriek. "WAAAAAACK!" cried whatever Catfish had or had him. There were more yelps and more waaaacks, not to mention hissing sounds.

It wasn't Charles Manson or liberal Democrats.

It was a lion that had escaped from the circus.

Either that or some alien thing with big claws and eyes.

Later I would recall the Jerry Clower story where a fellow climbed up a tree and met some sort of alien thing with big eyes and claws during a hunting trip.

"Shoot this thang!" the fellow cried to his friends.

"We're afraid we might shoot you," somebody said from the ground.

"Well," replied the man in the tree, "just shoot up here amongst us, 'cause one of us has got to have some relief."

I was frightened.

I have no children. Catfish is my child, my boy, my most loyal friend.

Then a silence fell over my back-yard battlefield.

A few moments later, Catfish came loping up the steps and ran back inside. I could see blood on his mouth, but I didn't know if it was his or that of whatever it was with which he had tangled.

The next morning, I went to my back yard expecting God knows what.

I found a dead raccoon — a large dead raccoon.

It apparently had been trying to eat out of Catfish's food plate on the back porch when it was pounced upon by the rightful owner of the food plate.

So I'm looking for a dead-raccoon-in-the-yard removal service, and I apologize to any of my neighbors who might have been disturbed.

Stephen King probably could write an entire novel based on such an experience. As for me, I'll just end it here and hope for a good night's sleep after the Night of the Killer Lab.

An Exchange of Brief Remarks

THERE WAS A LETTER CONCERNING ME ON THE EDITORIAL page of the Atlanta *Constitution* recently. It didn't take me long to figure out that the letter writer wasn't digging the viewpoints I often express.

She called me a redneck, a backward Southerner, a racist, a homophobe, a sexist, and I got the idea she didn't like it when I occasionally point out "yankees" (her quote marks, not mine) aren't always correct, especially when they tell us how they used to do it back in Buffalo.

I can take all that, but what got to me about this letter was the part where she said I was the "equivalent of dirty underwear dragged out to the living room by the family dog in front of company."

This is my fifteenth year writing a column and never before has anybody ever compared me to dirty underwear, the kind the dog drags out in front of company or otherwise.

And, just for the record, my dog Catfish, the black Lab, has never dragged out any dirty underwear in front of company in my house.

He has dragged out shoes, the scraps of last night's dinner from the garbage, and once he came into the living room—where I was listening to two women who wanted to talk to me about becoming a Jehovah's Witness — with an empty beer can in his mouth.

"Dog's got a serious drinking problem," I said to the two women.

"And about half drunk, he tends to get mean. Last week he got hammered and bit two guys trying to convince me to become a Mormon."

The two women were out the door a heartbeat later. Catfish just can't stand door-to-door religious soliciting. He also growls whenever he sees evangelists on television.

The reason it bothers me to be compared to dirty underwear is because my mother's greatest fear in life was that I would be in some sort of accident and I would be wearing dirty underwear and the doctors in the emergency room would see it.

"What kind of mother would they think I am if you were in a wreck and were wearing dirty underwear?" she often asked.

She never mentioned a word about my getting multiple head injuries or a broken neck in a wreck. As long as my underwear was clean, I suppose she figured I eventually would heal, and she would be off the hook as a lousy mother.

But as a result of that upbringing I would like to point out a couple of things here:

1. I never wear dirty underwear. If I get out of the shower and find I have no clean underwear, I get in my car, go to the store and buy a new pair. Rather than put on a pair of dirty underwear to go to the store, I don't wear any at all,

and I drive very carefully. I don't want those emergency room doctors to think I'm some sort of sicko-kinko.

2. I don't put my dirty underwear where my dog can get to it and drag it into the living room in front of company. I throw it in the closet and close the door, and even if I left it in a pile on the floor, Catfish is a class act who has a lot more things to do than drag out a pair of dirty underwear in front of company.

Like keeping me safe from religious fanatics and transplanted Yankees who occasionally knock on my door and ask if I know where they can get a good bargain on a grits tree.

Catfish the Lab Has Up and Died

MY DOG CATFISH, THE BLACK LAB, DIED THANKSGIVING night.

The vet said his heart gave out.

Down in the country, they would have said, "Lewis's dog up and died."

He would have been 12 had he lived until January.

Catfish had a good life. He slept indoors. Mostly he ate what I ate. We shared our last meal Tuesday evening in our living room in front of the television.

We had a Wendy's double cheeseburger and some chili.

Catfish was a gift from my friends Barbara and Vince Dooley. Vince, of course, is the athletic director at the University of Georgia. Barbara is a noted speaker and author.

I named him driving back to Atlanta from Athens where I had picked him up at the Dooleys' home. I don't know why I named him what I named him. He was all curled up in a blanket on my back seat. And I looked at him and it just came out. I called him, "Catfish."

I swear he raised up from the blanket and acknowledged. Then he severely fouled the blanket and my back seat.

He was a most destructive animal the first three years of his life. He chewed things. He chewed books. He chewed shoes.

"When I said to Catfish, 'Heel,'" I used to offer from behind the dais, "he went to my closet and chewed up my best pair of Guccis."

Catfish chewed television remote control devices. Batteries and all. He chewed my glasses. Five pairs of them.

One day, when he was still a puppy, he got out of the house without my knowledge. The doorbell rang. It was a young man who said, "I hit your dog with my car, but I think he's OK."

He was. He had a small cut on his head and he was frightened, but he was otherwise unhurt.

"I came around the corner," the young man explained, "and he was in the road chewing on something. I hit my brakes the second I saw him."

"Could you tell what he was chewing on?" I asked.

"I know this sounds crazy," the young man answered, "but I think it was a beer bottle."

Catfish stopped chewing while I still had a house. Barely.

He was a celebrity, Catfish. I spoke recently in Michigan. Afterward a lady came up to me and said, "I was real disappointed with your speech. You didn't mention Catfish."

Catfish used to get his own mail. Just the other day the manufacturer of a new brand of dog food called "Country Gold," with none other than George Jones's picture on the package, sent Catfish a sample of its new product. For the record, he still preferred cheeseburgers and chili.

Catfish was once grand marshall of the Scottsboro, Alabama, "Annual Catfish Festival." He was on television and got to ride in the front seat of a police car with its siren on.

Oh, that face and those eyes. What he could do to me

with that face and those eyes. He would perch himself next to me on the sofa in the living room and look at me.

And love and loyalty would pour out with that look, and as long as I had that, there was very little the human race could do to harm my self-esteem.

Good dogs don't love bad people.

He was smart. He was fun. And he loved to ride in cars. There were times he was all that I had.

And now he has up and died. My own heart, or what is left of it, is breaking.

COLLEGE FOOTBALL—THE OTHER SOUTHERN RELIGION

Georgia on My Mind

THERE ARE THOSE WHO WOULD LIKE TO SEE ALL THIS COME to an end. All this is 90,000 people showing up to see a football game between the University of Georgia and some other less prestigious institution of higher education on a beautiful fall Saturday afternoon.

Those who believe as I do will come in droves of red, down from the hills of Habersham, the valleys of Hall and up from the marshes of Glynn. They will be with friends and family. They will renew old acquaintances and return to the campus from which they sprang into real life.

But there are the naysayers. They see all this as detrimental to the lofty purpose of education. They are the pointy-heads, the nabobs, the ones who look at such an exercise as Neanderthal. They see only a game involving brawn and controlled violence. They don't see the real meaning, human beings living and loving a tradition that, in Georgia's case, is 100 years old.

So, I will tell them what my day will be like Saturday, and if they can still find something wrong with it, then they are hopeless.

I've been staying with the same friends on Athens football weekends long enough to know I'm always welcome in their home. After a slow morning of anticipation, we'll be in our parking place near the stadium at least a couple of hours before kickoff. Friends will come by. Football season is the only time we see some of them. It is what we have in common. It is what brings us together. We'll drink a beer and munch a bunch of wonderful chicken fingers.

I'll look at the bridge behind the stadium that separates the Old Campus from the New Campus. I walked a thousand miles crossing that bridge, starting in 1964. I was better on the Old Campus, incidentally. That's where they taught English and history and journalism. I could deal with those.

The New Campus, however, is where they tried to teach me botany. I made one C in college. It was in botany. I figured God was why trees grow, so I didn't take botany very seriously. When I think of all that, I'll be 21 again for a few precious moments. I'll still be basically innocent, and I'll still be married to a pretty blonde I fell in love with in grade school.

The arthritis in my right hand, the slightly balding spot on the back of my head and my schedule for the next week will jar me back to reality and the present. Then the game. We will bask in the glory of a Georgia touchdown. We will sink into our seats at any opponent's advantage.

It will be five hours of love and caring and dedication, and we will do it from September until November, and anybody who doesn't like it can go sit in the library and read about the Punic Wars. Just let me have this time. It is the best time that I live.

Another Kind of Hunting Season

IT WAS ALL OVER THE SUNDAY PAPER ABOUT THE RECRUITING of young athletes to play football at large universities in the region. It's that season. Children are snatched away from their mothers' arms back home in Twobit County, and the next thing you know, the Head Coach is saying, "Ol' Dram Bowie from down in Twobit County is the finest prospect I've ever seen."

Recruiting is important. "You gotta have the horses," a coach once told me, "before you can pull the wagon." Coaches talk like that. Translated, it means if he doesn't get off his tail and sign some talent, he'll be selling tires at Kmart the next time toe meets leather.

What I hear is that Tennessee is making a big move into Georgia in search of recruits to rebuild the once-mighty Volunteers program. You don't sign to go to Knoxville. You are sentenced there. Clemson is also usually heavy into seeking Georgia material. A Clemson raid makes Georgia Tech people especially mad.

"You know that tractorcade this weekend?" one asked me.

"They weren't farmers," he said. "They were Clemson fans on their way to Sears to buy clothes for the Gator Bowl."

From various sources around the Southeast, I have come into possession of the list of the most-wanted high school athletes in the state. None has signed yet. They are known as "blue-chippers" to the alumni. Coaches call them "job-savers." Here's the list.

ARDELL GROVER—Linebacker from Atlanta. Missed half his senior season with terminal acne. "He'll hit you," say the recruiters. Especially if you call him "Zit Head," which a tenthgrader did shortly before Ardell rendered him unconscious during fifth-period study hall.

MARVIN PALAFOX—Marvin is a tight end. He's from Macon. Wears No. 82. Scored same number on his college boards. "Great hands," say the coaches. So do the cheer-leaders.

SCOOTER T. WASHINGTON—Halfback from Savannah. Olympic speed. Expensive tastes. Wants two Cadillacs and a mink coat like Reggie Jackson's to sign. Answers the telephone, "You need the loot to get the Scoot." Contact through his agent, Sam the Fly, at the Wise Owl Pool and Recreation Hall, Savannah.

BILLY BOB WALTON—Offensive tackle from Moul-trie. Extremely offensive. Friends call him "Dump Truck" because that's how big he is, and he could eat all the pork chops and mashed potatoes out of the back of one. Made *Tifton Gazette* All-Area team. Makes Junior Samples look like David Niven. Loves buttermilk but can't spell it.

LAVONNE "The Rolling Stone" LARUE—Led Columbus high school in interceptions. Also led burglary ring to back entrance of Harry's One-Stop Stereo Shop.

Got one to five, but sentence suspended when entire student body turned out as character witnesses after suggestion they do so by several of The Stone's "acquaintances." "Can start for any college team in the country," says his coach, who didn't start him once and still carries the scars.

IRVING BOATRIGHT III—Quarterback for a fashionable northside Atlanta private school. Father prominent Atlanta attorney with homes on Hilton Head and Sea Island. Can't play a lick, but the head coach gets free legal advice and either house three weeks each summer. Started every game during high school career. Bed-wetter.

BARTHANATOMAY RIMJOB—Place-kicker. Son of Pakistani professor of Eastern philosophy at Clayton Junior College. Kicks soccer style. Made 110 straight extra points during prep career. Does not speak English and goes through 15-minute ancient ritual before every kick. Weighs 90 pounds soaking wet. Once scored winning touchdown on fake field goal by hiding ball in his turban.

ALBERT WARTZ JR.—From South Georgia. 6′ 4″, 250. Plays quarterback. Questionable student. Thinks Henry Cabot Lodge is a motel in Bainbridge. Filled out recruiting questionnaire. By "sex," wrote: "Not since Mavis Wilson moved out of Hahira." "This kid," says his high school coach, "doesn't know the meaning of 'quit.'" Doesn't know the meaning of third-grade arithmetic either. Leaning toward Alabama.

A Bear of a Man

I SPENT THE AFTERNOON DRINKING WITH PAUL BRYANT once.

I had been to Athens with him for an autographing session for the book he did with John Underwood of *Sports Illustrated.*

We returned to the old Atlanta Airport. There were still a couple of hours before his plane back home to Tuscaloosa.

"Let's get a drink," he said.

The weather was awful. Rain. High winds. Lightning and thunder. Bad flying weather. Good drinking weather.

He took me into the Eastern Ionosphere Lounge.

He ordered Double Black Jack and Coke. He ordered two at a time. I drank beer.

I probably got the best interview of my life. But I don't remember any of it. You can drink a lot of double Black Jack and Coke and beer in two hours.

I do remember leaving the lounge and walking to the Southern gate where his flight awaited, however.

At the gate, the Bear ran into a doctor from Tuscaloosa who was also booked on the flight. The doctor was also a part-time pilot.

"Coach," said the doctor. "I don't like this weather."

"You a drinking man, son?" Bryant asked him.

"Yes, sir," said the doctor.

"Well, let's go get a couple of motel rooms and have a

drink and fly home tomorrow."

There were 50 or so other would-be passengers awaiting the same flight to Tuscaloosa. When they noticed Bryant turning in his ticket, all but a handful did the same.

"If Bear Bryant's afraid to fly in this weather," a man said, "I ain't about to."

When the word came that Paul "Bear" Bryant, had died, I immediately thought of a friend of mine. She first met Bear Bryant several years ago. At first their relationship was purely professional. But it grew past that. I'm not talking about hanky-panky here, however. Grandfather-granddaughter comes the closest to describing how they felt about each other.

They were an unlikely pair. He the gruff, growling, old coot of a football coach. She a bright, young, attractive woman with both a husband and a career and with a degree from the University of Texas, of all places.

He would call her even in the middle of football season, and they would talk, and he would do her any favor. Once, a friend of hers, a newspaper columnist, was having heart surgery.

She called the Bear and had him send the columnist a scowling picture with the autograph, "I hope you get well soon—Bear Bryant."

The picture still hangs in the columnist's home.

I called her the minute I heard the news. I didn't want her to get it on the radio.

She cried.

"I loved him," she said. "And he loved my baby."

My friend had a baby a few years back. Had it been a boy she would have named him for the Bear. David Bryant. But it was a girl, and she was called Marissa.

"I had no problems with naming my son 'David Bryant,' but I wasn't about to name a little girl 'Beara,'" said my friend.

Of course, a busy big-time college football coach like Bear Bryant didn't give it a second thought that somebody else's little girl wasn't named for him.

He still sent her gifts. Gifts like a child's Alabama cheerleader uniform, and then an adult-size uniform for use later. He sent her footballs, dolls and probably a dozen or so letters that her mama read to her.

It's funny, though. When he sent his packages and letters, he always addressed them not to Marissa, but "To Paula."

Jealous Losers Name Them "Bubba Games"

SO IT HAS BEGUN. WRITERS IN OTHER PARTS OF THE COUNTRY have targeted Atlanta as Spartanburg with skyscrapers and are referring to the 1996 Olympics here as the Bubba Games. The ignorant dolts.

All this reminds me of the time in Chicago I met a young woman sitting on a bar stool next to mine. "Where are you all from?" she honked, mockingly, after I spoke.

"Atlanta," I said.

"I've always wondered," she went on, "if there were any nice restaurants out there?" Realizing at this point I was speaking to a Midwestern bimbo who had never been past Gary, Indiana, and realizing that if she were the last woman on earth, I'd rather change the spark plugs on my pickup than involve myself with her in any way, I corrected her on a few things.

"First of all, Thunderthighs," I began, "in the South we never use 'you all' in the singular sense. When referring to one as you did with your snippy little remark about my origins, you should have used a simple 'you.' When we refer to more than one person, we don't say 'you all' either. We say 'y'all.' Is that clear, Snowbrain?" She seemed startled. She had stopped chewing her gum.

"As to your question about there being any nice restaurants 'out there' in Atlanta, it is apparent you know as much

about geography as you know about fashion. Nice sweat-
shirt. New York is 'over there,' Milwaukee 'up there,' Los
Angeles 'out there.' Atlanta is 'down there.' As far as nice
restaurants are concerned, you'd be amazed how many there
are in Atlanta.

"It is a cosmopolitan, modern city, with paved roads and
indoor plumbing, and we don't have to put up with gray
snow and Arctic temperatures six months out of the year.
Now, if you'll excuse me," I ended, "I'm going back to my
apartment and call somebody in Atlanta so I can say I've
had at least one intelligent conversation today."

Atlanta has a world-class airport, and world-class hotels
and restaurants, and it will offer the 1996 Olympians
world-class facilities. What it won't offer is an opportunity
for journalists around the country to travel 5,000 miles on
expense accounts to some foreign site where they can
impress their friends and colleagues with a dateline from
somewhere their friends and colleagues have never been.

Instead of flying to someplace that sounds great until
you get there and find it crowded, overpriced and rude,
they'll be flying on expense accounts to Atlanta, a model
city for race relations, a vibrant city that can flat get it done
when it has to and a friendly city that very few visitors
leave without some measure of regret that their time here
is over.

Someone said Barcelona has cathedrals and Atlanta has
strip joints.

How many sports writers have ever been to a cathedral? Whoever it was who wrote that a dried cow pie might be used in Atlanta as a discus is full of the undried version. Will the heathens ever learn the worn out Bubba stereotype is not applicable to Atlanta and to much of the rest of the South? Probably not.

Boldly Standing Tall

I GOT HOOKED ON BASEBALL STANDINGS ABOUT THE SAME time I learned to tie my shoes. I would have been about 8. It's embarrassing to admit I didn't learn to tie my shoes until I was 8, but manual dexterity has never been my long suit and as soon as I got out on my own, I never bought another pair of lace-up shoes.

I'm a loafer man, and what this has to do with baseball standings I don't know, but the Braves just beat the Dodgers 10-3 and today is another great standings morning.

When I was 8, I was a great fan of the Atlanta Crackers, this city's entry into the AA Southern Association. When my aunt and uncle came home from the Moreland Knitting Mill for lunch during baseball season, they would bring along the morning paper and I would take it into my hands as something precious — like a puppy or a pork chop. I would turn immediately to the sports page and the baseball standings.

We couldn't get the Cracker radio broadcast in Moreland, 40 miles from Atlanta, so this is how I got my baseball news. There were no superstations, no all-sports cable networks. I miss those days when the tension would build in me all morning, and the newspaper, not a talking head, would give me the good or bad news about my beloved Crackers.

I got away from staring at baseball standings in the late

1960s. The Crackers had ridden the last train out and had been replaced by the Milwaukee Braves. The Braves landed in Atlanta as a mediocre team and just got worse. Who wants to look at the standings when your team is at rock bottom? When the Crackers were here, the newspaper would put ATLANTA in bold type in the standings. When the Braves came, the practice continued. That is, until I became executive sports editor of the Atlanta *Journal* in the 1970s.

Who wanted to draw even more attention to the fact that the city's baseball team was in the deep cellar? I nixed the bold ATLANTA. But that was then and this is now, and I've gone back to staring at the standings. How neat they are. How mathematically precise. What a story they have to tell.

The baseball season has been going on for almost five months, and everything that has happened is reflected to the last decimal point in the standings. Sunday morning, Atlanta was still on top of the National League West, and I looked at the name and the corresponding numbers next to it.

It was like looking upon a great painting, a beautiful woman or where an ocean meets a mountain range. The standings said Atlanta was 3 1/2 up on Cincinnati, with the best winning percentage in Major League Baseball. I slipped on my loafers and walked on air the rest of the day.

THE HEART,
THE SOUL AND
COUNTRY GOLD

Pardon Me, Are You in the Mood?

I GOT OLD THE OTHER DAY. I ORDERED A GLENN MILLER tape off television. That's a sure sign the aging process has settled in for good. First of all, if you're not old, why are you still up at the hour they advertise musical tapes from the '40s while you're watching a black and white movie with Stewart Granger or a young Richard Widmark? It's either because you're not sleeping like you used to, or you can't run with the big dogs anymore out there in the neon arena.

And instead of listening to current musical offerings, you've gone and ordered a tape from your parents' generation because it's nostalgic, because you can understand the words when somebody sings, because Glenn Miller music never suggested killing anybody or anything, and because it reminds you of a time you actually knew what was going on in the world.

I wasn't born when Glenn Miller died, but I listened to his music as a child on the radio and I saw my late parents jitterbug to "In the Mood" once.

And I've seen "The Glenn Miller Story" about a thousand times on that same late-night television.

Jimmy Stewart was magnificent as Glenn Miller, and aren't all we lost males of divorce, now in the summer of our years, still looking for June Allyson in the Madonna era? So my Glenn Miller tape came in from Time-Life music.

The TV offer wasn't good in Nebraska, or was it New Jersey? I'm not certain why there's usually one state left out when they advertise things you can order on late-night television, but thankfully, they never seem to leave out Georgia.

I had to make a two-hour drive alone, and I decided that would be a perfect time to enjoy my tape for the first time.

There wouldn't be anybody younger than me in the car to ask "What on earth is that?" and to demand that I remove the tape and listen to a rock station, a practice that always makes me nervous and irritable.

I pulled onto the interstate. It was raining. Large trucks roared past me, leaving walls of water upon my windshield, something else that always makes me nervous and irritable.

Then my tape began.

The first selection was the immortal "In the Mood." It made me want to jitterbug like my mother and father, and I relaxed and forgot about the trucks.

Next was "Pennsylvania 6-5000." That was June

Allyson's New York telephone number in "The Glenn Miller Story" and Glenn was so smitten by her he wrote a musical piece about her telephone number.

Love was like that in the '40s. Today, there's too many digits in a phone number to write a love song about one. "Pennsylvania 1-800-485-6234."

The hits kept coming.

"Moonlight Becomes You." What a lovely thought.

"Sunrise Serenade." Soft and sweet.

"Don't Sit Under the Apple Tree." Lovers asking each other to be true until the war is over.

"Chattanooga Choo-Choo." I enjoyed the piece, but I cringed at the political incorrectness of "Pardon me, boy."

All the greats were there, including "Little Brown Jug," which set me to bouncing around in my seat.

A kid with an earring and his hat on backward passed me. He probably thought I was in rhythm with rapper "Booger Nose" and his recent hit, "I'm Gonna Kill Your Dog."

So, I'm old.

There are benefits, including being able to listen to non-violent music, being satisfied with a living room couch instead of a bar stool, and realizing I can make it on four or five hours sleep instead of the eight or nine of my youth.

And the young women will be calling me "mister." But I still believe I'll run into June Allyson one of these days, and she'll invite me to go sit under an apple tree.

Yo, June. I'm in the mood.

Cool as Country Gets?

LAS VEGAS. THIS TOWN ONCE BELONGED TO SINATRA. TO Sammy Davis Jr. To Dean Martin. To Hollywood.

But look what's happening now: Conway Twitty and George Jones have just left Bally's and Randy Travis has taken their place.

Others who've either just closed or who are just opening are Reba McIntyre, Lorrie Morgan, Doug Kershaw, Charlie Daniels and Dolly Parton.

It's Nashville West. Vegas entertainment is in boots and jeans and out of tuxedos.

The primary reason country plays so well here, and everywhere else, is that it is no longer a stepchild of American music.

Country is now the No. 1 selling music in this country, and it isn't just crossover stars like Garth Brooks who have done it.

Conway Twitty, who can plead to get a lost love back with the best of them, has been here, and George (Possum) Jones, whose voice even sounds like a steel guitar, was with him.

And Randy Travis. He brought back the traditional sound of country music when it was headed Lord-knows-where with too many rock-sounding licks and not enough twin-fiddle intros.

I'm playing a rather minor role in all this. Randy Travis is giving me a half hour to tell jokes at Bally's before he brings them to their feet with "On the Other Hand."

A couple of my boyhood friends, Danny Thompson and Dudley Stamps, were here with me for a couple of days and it was Dudley who surveyed this scene and asked, "What was that song about being country a long time ago?"

"'I was Country When Country Wasn't Cool,' by Barbara Mandrell," I, quite the country music expert, answered.

"You know something?" Dudley went on, "That's us. We were country when they would laugh at you for listening to it."

We were. I gave up on rock 'n' roll when the Beatles arrived, adopted country and have never looked back.

"Steve Smith had the best country jukebox I've ever heard," Dudley added.

Steve Smith's truck stop in Moreland was our gathering place as boys. You could get a great cheeseburger for a quarter, and I can still hear that jukebox filling the night with Ernest Tubb and Faron Young and Patsy Cline as we sat on the hoods of our cars in Steve's parking lot dreaming our dreams.

"I never thought back then," said Danny, "that three of us would be in Las Vegas one day with all these country acts and you would be on stage telling jokes."

Neither did I. But country music and three ol' boys from Moreland, Georgia, have come a long ways. Keep us humble and grateful.

Conway Left Them Begging for More

MY FRIEND RON HUDSPETH, WHO GAVE UP SPORTS WRITING to write about how to have a good time, probably has seen more live country music acts than anybody else who doesn't promote them for a living.

He also has met Willie Nelson, has been on Waylon Jennings's bus, and once had a beer in a booth with Tom T. Hall, one of my country music heros, in Tootsie's Orchid Lounge in Nashville.

For that reason, I always have valued his opinions on country music and he has often said of Conway Twitty, "Nobody can get down there and beg like Ol' Conway."

And country music has a lot of getting down there and begging in it, even the modern variety. Doesn't Billy Ray Cyrus do a great deal of pleading in "Achy Breaky Heart"? Country songs beg for forgiveness, beg for departed lovers to come back, beg for peace of mind.

It's why country touches a lot of us.

"Honey, just forgive me and come on back home so I don't have to toss and turn and stare at this ceiling no more."

A thousand country songs have been written on that one sentence.

But Conway. The very sound of his voice was a cry for relief. It exuded agony. It broke and cracked at just the right time.

Nobody could put forth two simple words — "Hello, darlin'" — and imply more pain than Conway Twitty.

Willie Nelson can get close with, "Well, hello, there," but it's still not Conway running upon his lost love and greeting her as pitifully and as humbly with "Hello, darlin'" before launching into that plea to return that hits the bottom of the belly of anybody who has ever been in that sorrowful place.

We lost Conway over the weekend. He was 59.

I've already mentioned one reason for his success, that ability of his to find our own pain. But there was something else Conway did late in his career that gave him tremendous appeal to female country music fans, especially those we'll say who were over 30. Those whose husbands were on the couch with a beer wondering why the Braves can't hit.

Conway appealed to their sexuality. He went after their sexual frustrations, forged by the Creator's little joke of making the male's sexual peak at 19 and the female's at 35. (I read that somewhere.) Do you think I'm kidding? OK, what about this Conway line: "Even with your hair up in curlers, I'd still love to lay you down." He wasn't talking about sprawling on the living room carpet for a rousing game of Monopoly.

How about, "There's a tiger in these tight fittin' jeans," and, "You can't call him a cowboy until you've seen him ride"?

And didn't Conway record "Slow Hands"? Never was

there a more suggestive song on a country label.

I was at a live Conway concert myself once. The over-30 female set flocked to the stage with flowers for Conway. I saw the over-50 set do the same once at a Frank Sinatra gig in New York in the '70s.

Conway had all that permed hair and that Elvis-like stare and snarl, having sprung from the same era, and he made his female fans feel he would, in fact, swim the Mississippi to satisfy their longings. Billy Ray or Garth can't touch that.

Conway Twitty was a sex symbol, perhaps country music's first, and I've got to believe the tears are flowing like — if this were a country song — warm, red wine as the man groans one last time: "Hello, darlin.'"

Medallions' Music
Is a Gift That Endures

WE HAD THE SWINGIN' MEDALLIONS FOR A PRE–GEORGIA–
Florida football game party on lovely Sea Island, Georgia,
home of the five-star retreat, The Cloister.

They come to the Georgia coast by the thousands annu-
ally for the game, played in nearby Jacksonville.

The Swingin' Medallions. I have asked often what, if
anything, endures? Well, the Swingin' Medallions and their
kind of music — my generation's music — has.

I first heard them sing and play in the parking lot of a
fraternity house at the University of Georgia in 1965. They
had the land's No. 1 rock 'n' roll hit at the time, the celebrated, "Double Shot of My Baby's Love."

That was so long ago. I'd never been married and my
father was living with me. He had appeared at my apartment one day after one of his long absences, hat in hand.

I gave him a bed. He got a job running a local cafeteria.
He paid his part of the rent out of what he would bring
home to eat each night from the cafeteria. I never had a better eating year.

We were strolling along the campus together and heard
the music. We went to the fraternity parking lot from
whence it came and listened for a half an hour.

Daddy said, "Marvelous music. Simply marvelous."

My daddy said the same thing about World War II.

"Marvelous war. Simply marvelous."

The major thought practically everything was marvelous, simply marvelous, except women who smoked. I'm not sure why he thought more of world wars than women who smoked. I never got to know the man that well.

The Swingin' Medallions at the party were one original and the sons of originals. How nice to see one generation pass down its music to another. That rarely happens.

What clean-cut, personable young men they were. They let the more celebratory join for a few numbers behind their microphones. There is something about a microphone and an amplifying system and a little see-through whiskey to bring out imagined musical talent.

They did "Double Shot" twice. And they played all the other great shagging sounds from the '50s and '60s.

Sure, I'll list a few of them: "Stand By Me." Haunting melody if you listen to it very closely. Will you just hang around, darling, even through the bad times?

"My Girl." The Temptations' finest, in my mind.

"Be Young, Be Foolish, Be Happy." The Tams's greatest hit. I know a lady who wants it sung at her funeral.

"It's funny about this kind of music," one of the younger Medallions was saying. "We play for people your age [high side of 40 and up] and we play a lot of high school proms. The kids like it as much as you do, and they think it's something brand new."

Compared to what rock 'n' roll became in the '70s, it's

tame music, soft music. It is music to which there are actually discernable words.

And, perhaps the best thing about it is, you can actually talk above it.

My generation hasn't given what others have been asked to give. We've been through no depressions or world wars, for instance. We've given you Bill and Hillary.

But we have left our music, the kind the South Carolina–based Swingin' Medallions still plays with great feeling and just the right amount of showmanship for a group that didn't riot when it was announced the bar was closing down at 10:30.

It was a nice party and nobody is young enough to jump in the pool anymore. Marvelous. Simply marvelous.

Country Willie
Has Forsaken His Heritage

I WAS A WILLIE NELSON FAN BEFORE MOST OF TODAY'S Willie Nelson fans ever heard of Willie Nelson.

If you still haven't heard of Willie Nelson, you are seriously out of touch, but I will explain anyway. He currently is one of country music's most celebrated artists, whose appeal crosses over to almost every sort of audience.

He even made a successful album of songs your parents snuggled to when they were kids. "All of Me" and "Springtime in Vermont," for example, were songs Willie sang on his album, "Stardust."

Yeah, I go way back with Willie. Back to when people would throw rocks at you and not invite you to their parties if you confessed to a musical leaning toward anything or anybody out of Nashville.

I first heard of him as a writer of music. Some terrific old songs: "Funny How Time Slips Away," "Crazy," "The Night Life."

But then Willie started singing, too, and listening to that rather odd style of his — he almost talks songs at times — became one of my steady habits.

Willie sang songs like "Bloody Mary Morning" and "Mountain Dew," but he was just another Nashville hayseed until something about him suddenly began to appeal to the masses. The rest is millions of dollars' worth of history.

I have seen Willie perform live on any number of occasions. Once, in the back yard of the White House. It was a Southern sort of occasion. They served corn bread and cold beer, and as Willie did "Georgia On My Mind," a friend of mine, a true son of the South, turned and whispered to me: "My great-great-grandfather was wounded at Gettysburg and had to walk all the way back home to Fayette County, Georgia, after the war. If he were here tonight, he'd think we by-God won it."

Another friend and I were into deep fascination with Willie late one evening in my friend's living room. The womenfolk had gone to bed.

We were listening to Willie's incredible rendition of the hymn, "Precious Memories." My friend, quite seriously, said to me: "Promise me something. Promise if I die before you do, you'll make sure somebody plays Willie Nelson singing 'Precious Memories' at my funeral."

I promised. And he promised to do the same for me.

"Thinking about Willie singing," said my friend, "sort of makes you look forward to it, don't it?" I need to go on with the point here, and this is it: When Willie left Nashville for Texas and proclaimed himself an "outlaw," that was OK by me.

When I went to a Willie Nelson concert in a big hall and the smell of smoke was deeper than the smell of beer, I figured: The times, they are a-changin'.

When I listened to hard rock creep into some of Willie's

used-to-be-classic country arrangements, I stood for that, too.

And when Willie grew a beard ("just to see what the rednecks would do"), tied on a headband and started wearing an earring, I accepted all that as well. If Willie Nelson wants to put odd things in his ears, or in his nose, that is his business.

But enough is enough, and designer blue jeans with Willie Nelson's name sewn onto a back pocket is enough. They are available — "Willie" jeans — I read the other day.

Think about it. Calvin Klein. Gloria Vanderbilt. Vidal Sassoon. And now, Willie Nelson, forever yours in designer denim. For the record, they used to call Willie Nelson "Country Willie."

Precious memories. How they linger.

EDITOR'S NOTE: "Precious Memories" was sung at Lewis Grizzard's funeral, not by Willie Nelson but by hundreds of friends, fans and family members.